TRACKING
Significant Achievement

Series editors: Shirley Clarke and Barry Silsby

PRIMARY MATHEMATICS

Shirley Clarke and Sue Atkinson

Hodder & Stoughton
A MEMBER OF THE HODDER HEADLINE GROUP

Also published in this series:
Tracking Significant Achievement in Primary English
Tracking Significant Achievement in Primary Science
Tracking Significant Achievement in the Early Years

Acknowledgement
Many thanks to the schools, teachers and their pupils who contributed samples of significant achievement for this book.

British Library Cataloguing in Publication Data
A catalogue record for this title is available from the British Library

ISBN 0 340 65480 5
First published 1996

Impression number	10	9	8	7	6	5	4	3	2	1
Year		1999	1998	1997	1996					

Filmset by Wearset, Boldon, Tyne and Wear.
Printed in Great Britain for Hodder & Stoughton Educational, the educational publishing division of Hodder Headline Plc, 338 Euston Road, London NW1 3BH, by Bath Press, Bath, Avon.

Tracking Significant Achievement in

PRIMARY MATHEMATICS

Contents

1 Tracking Significant Achievement

The purpose of this book

With the advent of the revised National Curriculum, the focus for teachers' ongoing assessment has been to look for **significant achievement**, as opposed to looking for *all* aspects of achievement, which had been the previous practice.

This book, one of a series of four on significant achievement, aims to establish a coherent and manageable framework for organising ongoing assessment in the classroom, in which significant achievement is the focus. The underpinning principles for this are:

◆ the assessment process must include the child, aiming for the child to become part of the evaluation process;
◆ the assessment process must enhance the child's learning and the teachers' teaching;
◆ all assessment processes should be manageable.

This chapter describes good assessment practice, from the planning stage to assessment and record-keeping. It deals with the issue of defining significant achievement and how to look for it and recognise it.

Chapter 2 looks at good assessment practice within the context of mathematics, and considers good practice in mathematics teaching, organisation and resource provision which will enable significant achievement to take place and to be recognised.

Chapter 3 provides a variety of examples of significant achievement, derived from teachers' work in the classroom, covering the range of age groups and the different aspects of significant achievement across Key Stages 1 and 2. It is hoped that, by the time you have read all these examples, you will have a very clear idea of what significant achievement in mathematics might look like.

Chapter 4 sets out typical stages of significant achievement in mathematics. The purpose of this is to provide basic guidance for teachers about which aspects of mathematics are most important and significant in a child's mathematical development.

Chapter 5 has a question-and-answer format, covering all the issues that arose in a series of courses and during trialling carried out with teachers. It is followed by a final chapter on 'Getting Started'.

Defining assessment and its purpose

Mary Jane Drummond (1993) has a definition of assessment which clearly describes the process as it takes place in the classroom. She sets it out as three crucial questions which educators must ask themselves when they consider children's learning. Those questions are:

◆ *What is there to see?*
◆ *How best can we understand what we see?*
◆ *How can we put our understanding to good use?*

'What is there to see?' refers to the fact that we need to be able to access children's understanding in the best possible way. We need to be constantly talking to children about their work and maximising the opportunities for them to achieve in the first place and demonstrate their achievement in the second.

'How best can we understand what we see?' is the next stage. We need to be able to create a climate in the classroom where teachers are not simply hypothesising about the reasons for children's understanding, but have as much information as possible about a child's understanding, coming from the child itself. We also need to be clear about

the learning intentions of every activity, so that we know what we are looking for. We need to be flexible, however, because a child's achievement is not always directly related to the aims of the actual lesson. We need to remember that children learn from all their experiences of life, of which school learning is only a part.

'How can we put our understanding to good use?' is the key factor in moving children forwards. If the teacher has answered the first two questions, then the information gathered should give clear indications as to what should be the next move in helping a child to continue to progress.

The purpose of the assessment process is to make explicit children's achievements, celebrate their achievements with them, then help them to move forward to the next goal. Without children's involvement in the assessment process, assessment becomes a judgmental activity, resulting in a one-way view of a child's achievement. Information gathered in this way has minimal use. When shared with the child, assessment information is more likely to result in a raising of standards, because the child is more focused, motivated and aware of his or her own capabilities and potential. Good assessment practice enables children to be able to fulfil their learning potential and raises self-esteem and self-confidence.

'Assessment' can sometimes be used as the term for what is, in fact, record-keeping. It needs to be made clear that the assessment process is that outlined so far: a means of understanding children's understanding. Record-keeping is a follow-up to the assessment process, and needs to take place only when significant achievement has taken place. This will be described in some detail later. Evidence-gathering is part of the follow-up to assessment, and should be centred round the idea of a 'Record of Achievement' rather than a 'collection of evidence'. It is neither a statutory requirement (see both DFE/DFEE and SCAA documentation) nor useful to keep samples of children's work at set points in time as proof of National Curriculum attainment, whereas Records of Achievement are a motivating and useful aspect of the assessment process.

The planning, assessment and record-keeping cycle: a practical solution

The pre-planning stage

If assessment is to be worthwhile, it is clear that we must first maximise the opportunities for children's achievement, by giving them the best possible learning experiences. This can be achieved by a number of support structures in a school and by planning well in advance of the teaching.

Most primary schools have a 'curriculum framework' showing specific coverage of the programmes of study for 'blocked' work (e.g. history, geography, science and sometimes maths topics). These charts show who will cover what and in what term. Knowing what it is you have to cover in this way aids planning and enables a school to set up resources of high quality in order to help teachers at the planning stage. Well managed, good quality topic boxes are an excellent idea, with the following as the ideal contents:

◆ artefacts, maps, charts, videos, reference books, tapes;
◆ teachers' previous plans;
◆ lists of local places to visit (e.g. nearby streets with good examples of Victorian houses) and museums, etc;
◆ lists of local facilities (e.g. loan packs from local libraries, etc);
◆ lists of people who can be used as a resource (e.g. artists in residence, local poets and historians, people who work in the school who have related interests and expertise);
◆ brainstorms of starting-point ideas for contextualising the topic (e.g. set up a shop in the classroom as a way of contextualising work on money).

With such resource support, teachers are more likely to create interesting, well-resourced topic plans, resulting in contexts in the classroom which enable children to learn more easily.

For ongoing aspects of the curriculum, such as language and maths, planning is focused much more around the scheme of work.

The planning stage

The single most important feature of good planning is to have well thought out learning intentions before any creation of activities. It is traditional practice in primary schools to have only the simplest notion of aims, then to launch into a brainstorm, resulting in a topic web of activities. Very often, it is the creation of so many activities which causes manageability problems for teachers. It can also lead to a ticklist approach, where getting through the activities is more important than responding to the way children react to them. It is children's learning which must be our main concern, *not* our plans or schemes of work. They should support the learning, not hinder it.

We suggest a method of planning which starts with clear learning intentions and leads to only a few activities, all of which can be developed in depth, resulting in less superficial learning and a less frantic approach to coverage:

1   Find out what the children already know about the area to be covered, by brainstorm, open-ended problem or concept mapping. Brainstorming can be done with any age group. Simply say *'Next term we will be finding out about shapes. What do you already know about shapes?'* The resulting brainstorm will provide vital planning information for the teacher: the differentiation range – from the child who has only the simplest notion of shapes, to the child who knows more about the subject than the teacher! Having this means that activities can be planned which will meet the needs of all the abilities in the class if the two extremes have been defined.

2   Read the Programme of Study (PoS) statements.

3   Divide the topic, if necessary, into sub-headings – maybe two or three.

4   Create learning intentions, as follows, for each sub-heading:
◆ knowledge (*What do I want the children to know?*)
◆ skills (*What do I want the children to be able to do?*)
◆ concepts (*What do I want the children to understand?*)
◆ attitude (*What do I want the children to be aware of?*)

◆ equal opportunities (*What do I want the children to be aware of?*)

Clearly, the last two learning intentions lend themselves much more to geography, history or science topics than to maths topics, say, so should be used where appropriate.

Considering first what you want the child to learn means that you are absolutely clear about the purpose of the tasks children will do – a crucial step towards being able to create an evaluative ethos in the classroom. If the teacher is not clear why children are doing a task, the activity is likely to produce superficial results and a feeling of anxiety on the part of the teacher, who may feel that she does not know exactly what she is supposed to be expecting or looking for.

Making assessments in the classroom: setting up the assessment dialogue

Once the teacher is sure of the purpose of every task, the next step is to let children into the secret! By this, I mean, in words which they will understand, say *why* you want them to do the activity (e.g. *'I want you to play this maths game because it will help you order your numbers to 100. I also want to see how well you can take turns.'*). This can be said to the whole class, a group, pairs or individuals, depending on how you set children off. The important thing about this is that it takes no more time than it does for the task itself to be explained; it simply needs to become a habit on the part of the teacher.

It is important that children are let into the secret for two reasons:

◆ First, because knowing the purpose focuses the child towards a particular outcome. Very often, children have no idea why they have been asked to do something, and they can only look for clues or 'guess what's in the teacher's mind' as a means of knowing what is expected of them.

◆ Second, because they are being invited to take more control over evaluating their achievements. If the purpose is known, this is more likely to encourage the child to be weighing up the relative strengths and weaknesses of their work as they are doing it.

With children informed of the purpose of the task, the assessment agenda has been set, because, when children finish their work, or are spoken to in the middle of the task, the teacher can say *'How do you think you have got on with ordering your numbers/taking turns?'* This does not mean that there should be a systematic attempt to speak to *every* child, as that would be unmanageable. Apart from setting children off and concluding a session, most of a teacher's time is spent talking to individual children, by going to see how they are getting on or by their coming to the teacher. So the time *does* exist when children can be asked about their progress. It does not need to be structured, set-aside time, but can become part of the ongoing dialogue teachers have with children all through the day. The 'assessment dialogue' is simply a *different* way of talking to the children. The advantage for the teacher in asking the children how they are doing in relation to the 'shared secret' or learning criteria is that it is a powerful strategy for accessing information about children's progress.

This type of questioning invites the child to play an active part in his/her learning. Children who are used to being asked such questions readily respond, giving honest answers, because they know the purpose of the teacher's questions is to help their learning process. The answers children give often put a teacher fully in the picture about the child's level of understanding, as well as why something now appears to be understood (e.g. *'I understand this now'*, *'Lisa helped me with these two'*, *'I didn't want to work with Sam because I wanted to do it like this'*, etc).

This is the assessment process at its best. It describes the means by which the teacher makes all her ongoing decisions about children's learning and what they need to do next. Most of the insights gleaned from this continuous dialogue simply inform day-to-day decisions and it is unnecessary to record them. However, when significant achievement occurs, there is a need to recognise and record the event.

Making assessments in the classroom: looking for significant achievement and recording it

Record-keeping must have a purpose. If a teacher is to spend time writing things down, it must be useful to both teacher and child. If record-keeping is focused on children's significant achievement, it fulfils many purposes. First, however, we need to look closely at what significant achievement is.

Significant achievement is any leap or development in progress; anything which a teacher feels is important enough to write down. It will not happen very often, or it could not be defined as significant. It may be the first time a child does something (e.g. sitting still for more than five minutes), or it may be when the teacher is sure that a particular skill or concept has now been thoroughly demonstrated (e.g. in a number of contexts, shows an understanding of place value). Work with teachers has led us to believe that significant achievement falls into five categories:

◆ **physical skill** (e.g. use of scissors);
◆ **social skill** (e.g. able to take turns);
◆ **attitude development** (e.g. increased confidence in problem-solving);
◆ **concept clicking/conceptual development** (e.g. clear understanding that multiplication is repeated addition);
◆ **process skill** (e.g. able to generalise).

These are all examples of possible significant achievement in the context of mathematics. Clearly, what is significant for one child is not necessarily so for another. This is a welcome departure from the style of assessment which puts a set of arbitrary criteria, rather than the child's own development, as the basis of one's judgements. However, National Curriculum criteria are still considered, because the programmes of study have formed the basis of the planned learning intentions.

The more examples of significant achievement one sees, the clearer the idea becomes. If a child is a relatively slow learner, it does not mean that the child will have no significant achievement. It simply means that significance has to be redefined for that child. For instance, a child who takes six months to learn how to count to 5 will have a number of significant events leading up to this (e.g. the first time she can say the numbers, attempting to count objects without one-to-one correspondence, being able to count to 5 with one-to-one correspondence, being able to count to 5 objects regardless of their relative size, etc). Similarly, a child who always does everything perfectly needs to be given more challenging, problem-solving activities in order to demonstrate significant achievement.

The *context* within which significant achievement can be spotted is usually the ongoing assessment dialogue, although it may be demonstrated by a product, such as a piece of writing the child has done. When significant achievements occur, they can be underplayed in a busy classroom. Children have the right to have *all* their significant achievements recognised, understood and recorded. Recognition consists of simply informing the child (e.g. *'Well done, that is the first time you have set your work out neatly'*).

Understanding *why* the significant event took place is a crucial part of this process. It consists of asking the child *why* the significance occurred. In trialling with teachers, we found that the child's answer often contradicts what the teacher saw as the reason for the significant achievement. This is an important discovery, because it shows that we must find out, from the child, *why* the significant achievement occurs if we are to be able to follow up the achievement with appropriate teaching strategies. One example of a piece of work brought to a course on significant achievement demonstrates the importance of finding out why the achievement took place:

❢ *Ben chose for the first time to be a scribe in shared writing. Shared writing had been going on for over a year, with children in pairs, so this was significant for Ben. The teacher believed that this had happened because of the context of the story ('Horrible Red Riding Hood' – from the wolf's point of view), and her decision was to do more 'reverse' fairy stories as a way of encouraging Ben. However, when asked to go back and ask Ben why he had done this, the teacher reported that Ben said 'It was because you put me with Matthew, and he's shy, like me.' The implications for the teacher now are considerably different. Clearly Ben is sensitive to the dominance of the child he is working with, and the teacher's way forward now is to consider his pairing more carefully, both for writing and perhaps for other curriculum areas.* **9**

The child should be central to the recognition and recording of the comment. During the course of a lesson, when the achievement occurs, the teacher, in a one-to-one situation, needs to make much of the event (e.g. *'Well done, Ben. This is the first time you have. . . . Tell me why this happened'*).

Models of recording significant achievement

In trialling this approach, we decided that any teacher records made should as far as possible be in the possession of the child, in order to have the most impact on the child's learning.

Two main types of achievement were identified: where it relates to a **product** (piece of work, drawing, etc) and where it relates to an **event**, with no accompanying work. The following list outlines the features of good, manageable, formative comments which would appear on the child's actual work, or, if it is an event with no product, on a separate piece of paper which is then slotted in to the child's Record of Achievement:

◆ the date
◆ *what* was significant
◆ *why* it was significant

An example of a comment for significant achievement:

6 *Ben chose today, for the first time, to be the scribe in shared writing. Ben said he was able to do this because he was working with Matthew, who is quiet, like him.* **9**

A typical child's tray of work or exercise books, then, would have traditional comments on most of the pages (e.g. *'Well done, Ben'*) and occasional comments *about* the child whenever significant achievement has occurred. The formative comment has many benefits:

◆ The child 'owns' the comment and has witnessed it being

written, having been asked to say why the significant achievement took place.

◆ Parents and other interested parties find it much more meaningful to focus on the times when a significant formative comment has been written, because they make the progression of the child explicit.

◆ The child and teacher can look back to previous comments at any time, to compare with further progress and to help know what needs to be targetted for the future.

The Record of Achievement

The Record of Achievement is the place where any notable work is placed. The work should be negotiated between the teacher and the child. Unlike previous 'evidence collections', there is no systematic approach when using a Record of Achievement. It is simply an ongoing collection of any special work done by the child, and has been proved to be a highly motivating aspect of assessment. The Record can contain work or other measures of achievement from both inside and outside the school. Its main purpose is to motivate the child and impact on progress. Unlike the more traditional approach to Records of Achievement, the *teacher*, and not the child, is the main manager of the Record, negotiating with the child and gradually helping him/her to be able to identify significance for him/herself.

Summary

There are two places, then, where comments are written and placed when significant achievement takes place. **Written work or other products** have the comment written onto them and stay in the child's tray, or may be photocopied and placed in the child's Record of Achievement. **Event-style or non-product significant achievement** (e.g. organising a group of children) has the comment written on a piece of paper (perhaps with a decorated border) which is then placed in the child's Record of Achievement. These records should be accessible to the child, not locked away and owned by the teacher. The ideal system is to have concertina folders in a box in the classroom.

Some teachers find that there are too many pieces of paper

involved in *non-product* sheets, so prefer to record achievements in a single booklet for each child. This booklet is stored in the child's Record of Achievement and the child is simply asked to bring it to the teacher when something new is to be recorded. References to *product*-style achievements (e.g. *'See Danny's science work on 16 February'*) can also be made in this booklet or on separate sheets, so that there is then a one-to-one correspondence with all the significant achievements for a child and the number of references in the Record of Achievement. Keeping the comment in the child's exercise book or work, without placing it in the Record of Achievement, however, has been found to be just as effective in motivating children. The most important thing is that children's achievements are explicitly recognised and a recording made.

In order to be able to easily access significant achievements in children's workbooks, some teachers place a coloured sticker in the top right-hand corner of the page where the comment had been made. This is not a 'praise' sticker, but simply a marker, which is very effective for being able to see progression quickly, and is especially useful for parents and writing reports.

The summative tracking system

So far, we have described the process of assessment and the accompanying formative record-keeping. However, so that the system is rigorous and children do not fall through the net, there needs to be some kind of summative tracking system. This should not be a burdensome task, so we suggest the following simple mechanism: each half-term, term, or perhaps for a whole year, the teacher takes an A3 sheet of centimetre-squared paper, or similar, and writes the children's names down the side and the contexts in which significant achievement might occur along the top. These would be, essentially, the teaching contexts. For example: Reading/Writing/Number/Shape and Space/Science topic/etc). The headings could also include the foundation subjects, but the statutory requirement is that records of some kind must be kept for the core subjects only. Bearing in mind our definition of significant achievement, however, it would seem appropriate to include all the teaching contexts, or perhaps have a further heading which simply says 'Other contexts'. A teacher in the early years would probably have different headings, such as Play/Role Play/Sand and Water/Constructional Play or Creative, Aesthetic, etc. Then, when significant achievement occurs, and the teacher has written the brief formative comment, she keeps track of this by entering the date and a code to show which category of significance occurred (see Figure 1).

Names	Speaking & listening	Reading	Writing	Number	Topic (Science etc.)	Other
Laura			8/2 ⓒ		16/3 Ⓐⓒ	4/2 Ⓐⓒ
Cassie	3/3 ⓈⒶ	14/2 Ⓐ	19/3 ⓒ	2/4 ⓒ	1/2 ⓅⓈ	15/3 Ⓐ
Peter	4/2 ⒶⓈ	18/3 Ⓐ	21/2 ⒶⓅⓈ	1/3 Ⓐⓒ	16/3 ⓅⓈ	3/4 ⓈⒶ
Roxanne		21/4 ⓒ	21/4 ⓈⒶ	17/3 ⓅⓈ		
Sam	3/3 ⓅⓈ				17/3 ⓒ	
Dean	12/1 Ⓐ	10/3 Ⓐ	28/3 Ⓐⓒ	17/1 ⓅⓈ	11/3 Ⓟ	2/4 Ⓟ
Jenny	8/2 Ⓢ	8/2 ⒶⓅⓈ	4/1 ⓒ	9/3 ⓅⓈ	20/3 ⓒ	11/3 ⒶⓈ
Danny			18/3 ⓒ		6/2 ⓅⓈ	9/3 ⒶⓈ

Ⓐ Attitude development   ⓒ Conceptual development   Ⓟ Physical Skill
ⓅⓈ Process skill   Ⓢ Social skill

Figure 1

This tracking record can serve a number of functions. At a glance the teacher may see:

◆ a few children who appear to have shown no significant achievement, and therefore need to be focused on, in case they have been missed because they are quiet;
◆ a child who has shown significant achievement in, say, reading, but not in writing, and who therefore needs to be checked;
◆ the fact that none of the children has shown any significant achievement in, say, science, which indicates a need for the teacher to rethink the curriculum on offer;

Yr 2 Name	Speaking / listening	Reading	Writing	Number	Topic	Other
Cassie	(S)(A) Took quite a complicated verbal message, and was able to deal with a query and bring back an answer.	(A) Is now choosing to read 'chapter' books.	(C) Writing consistently with correct sentence formation.	(C) Understanding concept of X and knows 2/5/10 tables – with understanding.	(PS) During experiment about light in relation to seeds. 'How can we water the ones that we have to keep covered?' (in the dark).	(A) Able to cope with 'not knowing' how to do something. She can now accept a challenge.
Peter	(A)(S) Co-operating with a partner to prepare for class assembly, and behaving in an appropriate manner during assembly.	(A) Avidly 'reads' books on the carpet, at the start of the school day.	(A)(P)(S) Sitting quietly and persevering with his improved handwriting.	(A)(C) Devising assorted maths problems with common answer (ways to make 8), he really persevered.	(PS) Seeds/light experiment. 'Put one lot of seeds up on the shelf – in the shade. (My Nan has a plant that doesn't get much light, it's in the hall.)'	(S)(A) Managing to play sociably with other children during playtime.
Dean	(A) Related own story, coherently, to ancillary.	(A) Enjoying using picture dictionaries to aid word recognition.	(A)(C) Can spell SPACE – verbally and written (other spelling very poor).	(PS) Was able to identify the need for string to aid measurement in a 'maze' problem.	(P) Made excellent – unaided – junk and clay models of a rhino.	(P) Persevering with learning to skip – he can do it!
Jenny	(S) Leading a small group discussion whilst making a group poster.	(A)(PS) Reading with good comprehension – completed task related to her reading.	(C) Use of common spelling patterns – what, which – who – when.	(PS) Independently solved 'maze' problem by using variety of measuring mediums – found that thread was easiest.	(C) Demonstrated reason for shadow disappearing/re-appearing when body moves into a shadow.	(A)(S) Giving spontaneous praise to a child with low self-esteem.

Figure 2

◆ a bright child who appears to have shown no significant achievement, which indicates that he/she needs to be given more challenging, open-ended tasks.

One teacher in her second term of tracking significant achievement found that, on average, she recorded six comments per child in a half-term. Figure 2 shows some of these (these comments were written on the child's work or event sheet, and have only been reproduced in this way for the purpose of this book).

End-of-year records

Anything passed on to the next teacher needs to be useful to that teacher and able to be read quickly and easily. It is of no use passing on the whole Record of Achievement, because much of the content would have served its purpose and been surpassed by subsequent pieces of work. Good practice, therefore, is to sift the contents down to the last four pieces of significant work – say, one story, one account, one maths investigation and one science investigation. This will be manageable and useful for the next teacher to read. In the case of children with particular learning difficulties, it may be useful to pass on more pieces, perhaps showing the progression across the year.

As well as these pieces, the standard items passed on through the school would accompany them (e.g. reading record, end-of-year report, perhaps 'best fit' National Curriculum levels for each child in the class). Teachers involved in trialling this system felt it unnecessary to pass on the summative tracking matrix, because this is essentially a working document.

Conclusion

This chapter outlines a framework for assessment which would first and foremost put the child's learning and development first. However, **this system can also meet the statutory requirements**. The following chapters have been carefully constructed to build on this chapter; giving examples of significant achievement, defining it within mathematics itself, and answering the most common questions which teachers ask about looking for significant achievement.

Teachers, in trialling, were inspired and delighted by the fact that, at last, with this system, they could make the focus of their assessment practice the total development of the child, where **equal status is given to tiny steps, which might otherwise be seen as trivial, and more traditional demonstrations of progress.** The feedback has been, overall, that although it takes a while to get used to this different approach, the impact on the children's self-esteem and progress, the working atmosphere in the classroom, and children's ability to evaluate and set their own targets is considerable and, for some children, has resulted in leaps in progress which teachers have said would not otherwise have occurred. In their first summer after using tracking significant achievement, teachers said that their end-of-year records had never been easier to write.

It seems appropriate to end with some work from a child (Figure 3). The teacher asked the children, after their first term of focusing on significant achievement, to write a summary of their improvement. I believe that this child's account of his progress (and other accounts were all in the same vein) illustrates perfectly the emphasis that this philosophy places on the whole child, rather than just school-based learning.

Reference

Drummond, M.J. (1993) *Assessing Children's Learning*, David Fulton Publishers.

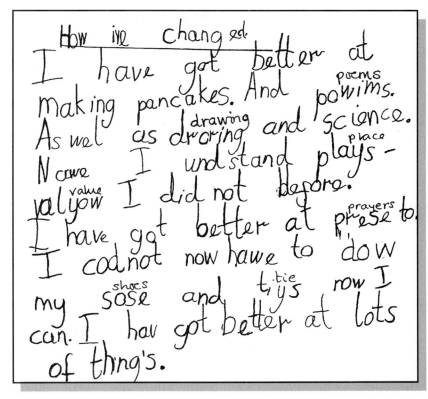

Figure 3

2 Supporting Significant Achievement in Mathematics

Why teach mathematics?

Three general principles held about the importance of teaching mathematics to children are:

◆ that mathematics provides a means of communication which is powerful, concise and unambiguous;
◆ that being able simply to manipulate symbols and follow procedures is, in itself, not useful, but the ability to apply mathematical skills and concepts is a vital tool in real life, for solving problems, both numerical and otherwise;
◆ that there is a creative, aesthetically pleasing element of mathematics when it is explored for its own sake.

The mathematics in the National Curriculum of England and Wales and the 5–14 Guidelines in Scotland reflect these principles and recommendations, and advocate teaching maths in such a way that children learn to think for themselves. There is consistent emphasis on problem-solving (in which maths is set in a context that children understand and which relates to real experiences) and investigative maths (in which there is an open-ended starting point and children explore the problem in their own way and come up with their way of doing it).

The various curricula clearly support the view that children learn maths best when they are using their *own* methods of calculating, so mental methods are encouraged and children are taught to develop their own intuitive methods of working rather than only being taught standard written algorithms. The National Curriculum requires that various operations should be taught, but methods and algorithms are not specified.

For some years there has been a growing awareness of the need to counteract the widespread view of maths as something that is about fear and failure. Many adults report their own low level of confidence with maths, so it is reasonable to assume that developing positive attitudes in our children will contribute towards their future success with maths.

What do we know about learning maths?

There has been a considerable amount of research about the ways in which children learn maths. The following points summarise this research:

1   Children learn maths by doing it and by talking about it.

2   Language is integral to all secure mathematical learning, so the talking is crucial.

3   When children are encouraged to use their own methods for calculating, their maths improves significantly.

4   When children have access to computers and calculators, they can develop and explore maths that they would otherwise not have access to. (The calculator becomes a tool to explore decimals at age 7 for example, something we would have thought impossible ten years ago, and through the use of Logo and floor turtles children can access and have control over their own mathematical thinking.)

5   It is children who have had the widest experience of maths in all sorts of different contexts who perform best on tests, not those given a restricted diet of arithmetic and book-oriented work.

6   Children do not seem to learn maths in a linear way, learning one thing after another. It is a complex process. They often learn things that we don't think we have taught them, and fail to learn things that we think we have taught them. Learning seems to resemble a jigsaw, with concepts clicking into place as new experiences inform previous experiences. What seems to be crucial in this process is finding out what the children already know and then trying

to build on that. This theory of learning is known as 'constructivism'.

7   There exists an ability range of no less than seven years (the 'seven year gap') by the time children are eleven years old, so a differentiated curriculum is vital. It is also impossible, therefore, to expect every child in a class to have achieved the same thing by the end of a year.

8   There should be a variety of teaching and learning styles, including exposition, discussion, practical work, consolidation and practice, problem-solving and investigational work (Cockroft 1982).

9   Very young children are capable of dealing with large numbers, even if they cannot give the exact value of each digit (PRIME).

10 Without being taught standard algorithms, children develop their own mental images of maths (e.g. many children develop a mental number line, and become extremely proficient at mental mathematics) (PRIME).

These points will be referred to throughout this book, as it is what we know about children's learning that is the key to effective teaching and our understanding of their achievements.

The implications for the classroom

Children's active role in their own learning

The crucial role of activity in maths cannot be over-emphasised. In classrooms where maths is mostly about writing things down and about doing standard algorithms from the board or textbook, there is clear evidence that the actual understandings of these children is very much lower than in classrooms where there is a greater emphasis on practical maths and on children using their own methods. In the first type of classroom children can do the maths – until it is put into a problem-solving context. This sometimes reveals severe weaknesses in understanding. For example, children don't know which operation sign to use, or they seem unable to apply the knowledge that they have just used in a page from a scheme.

It seems that the children with the widest curriculum and with less 'formal' arithmetic work actually do better in maths.

Language

Although activity in maths is crucial, it is equally important that activity is linked with an emphasis on language development. Many people believe that it is through language that we learn about mathematical concepts, and therefore, getting children to talk about their experiences and understandings in maths sessions, is a significant factor in the learning process. Many psychologists believe that talking is a crucial part of general cognitive development. In other words, talking contributes to children's learning (see Vygotsky 1971, Tizard and Hughes 1984 and Brissenden 1988):

6 *Theory and research in talk as a means of developing understanding support an intimate link between thought and language and suggest that concept formation and language development go hand in hand.* 9

(Tom Brissenden 1988)

As children discuss their work, it is possible for us to listen in and get some sense of what is going on in their heads. We can observe them groping their way towards a concept, as they try to explain what they mean (often as they manipulate apparatus). It is through this listening that we come to know what it is that the children are thinking. Without this knowledge we cannot find out what children already know, and we cannot find out where their misconceptions are. If we are to set up conditions in our class where children's conceptual development is given the optimum conditions for growth, we need to know what they know in order to build on that.

Here is an example of a teacher listening to a child, being given insight into what the child was thinking. Matthew was 6 and about to have his National Curriculum test. His teacher was going over subtraction with him and she wrote down

$$8 - 4 =$$

She asked him *'What is 8 take away 4?'*

Matthew said 8. She could have said 'wrong' and then showed him how to do it, but instead she asked him how he knew that. He put his hand over the 4 and said *'8 take away 4 leaves the 8'*.

We need to ask ourselves if our classroom organisation is such that children are working together on some of their tasks, communicating mathematically, and being given a sufficiently wide experience of talking about what they are doing. The implications of this are that we need to consider the place that we give to language in our maths lessons. If it does not have a high priority, perhaps we are not setting the conditions for significant achievement as well as we might. Some ways of giving 'talk' a higher priority are to:

◆ encourage child/child and child/teacher discussion;
◆ use group work and paired work where it is appropriate;
◆ use games in which saying what you are doing is an integral part of the rules.

The teacher's role is critical in making talk effective. Our interventions are crucial if we are to improve the ways in which children discuss their work, develop their thinking about what they are doing, and are encouraged to think for themselves. If we give out lots of information, have a class teaching strategy that focuses on 'telling' or 'explaining', it is possible that we might be talking too much and in the wrong kind of way. Examples of good questions and interventions are:

Can you tell me what you are doing?
Do you know why that happened?
What are you thinking about?
Do you think she is right?
What do you think?
What did you think of what Abdul said?

What if we . . . ?
Maybe you could try something different?
Would it work if you . . . ?
Can you find another way to do that?
That is such a good thought! Can you say it again?
Wow! That was terrific. Anyone want to add to that?
I don't know . . . let's find out.

One outcome of raising the status of talking in maths lessons is that it starts the crucial assessment dialogue between the teacher and the child – and once this gets going it is likely to spill over to the child and parent and to the parent and teacher.

It is that dialogue that we need to get started in our classrooms if we are to succeed in finding and recording significant achievements with our children.

Consider these two examples:

Example 1
(Teacher with two Year 1 children adding 39 to 42)

Teacher.	Can you tell me what you did?
Child 1.	I put them like this (pointing to cubes in groups of 10).
Teacher.	And what did you find out?
Child 1.	Seventy-one. There's seventy-one.
Teacher.	Can you tell me how you worked that out?
Child 1.	I did it, um, in tens like this; 10, 20, 30, 40, 50, 60, 70 and one more.
Teacher.	What about you, Gavin? Are you happy with that?
Child 2.	I wrote it down, Miss. Thirty-nine add forty-two. We done it . . . seventy-one.
Teacher	And how could you check to see you are right?

(The conversation went into a whole-class discussion.)

Example 2
Teacher.   What is this shape called?
Child 1.   It's like on that (pointing to a picture on a wall).
Teacher.   What is it called? (silence) A . . . a . . . tri . . . a . . . tri . . . ? A triangle. What is it?
Teacher and whole class.   A triangle.

(The discussion then moved on with no real discussion about the shape on the wall or what was special about triangles, or what the children understood by that word.)

It is in the first example that the teacher and child are in a real dialogue, where the teacher is seeking to understand what the child is thinking.

The type of task

Another condition for revealing significant achievement in the classroom is providing open-ended tasks that also require children to solve their own problems. It is clear that we cannot know whether a child can really understand something unless we engage the child in a problem-solving task in which the knowledge has to be applied.

It is one thing to 'understand' division and get all the 'sums' right on a page of a textbook where they are all division 'sums' and each one has the division sign beside it. But it is a totally different thing for a child to understand at the level of knowing which operation to use when faced with a real problem. For example, Gary (8), trying to work out how many large packets of crisps were needed for a class party if one packet could be shared between three people and there were 31 children in the class, looked at his calculator in a puzzled way and asked *'Do I need times or share?'* He tried both and was still puzzled, but a group of much less able children working with cubes said *'We need 11 packets and we'll have some left over.'*

The odd thing was that Gary could do division sums very much more confidently on paper than the other group.

He knew what to do if he was told what to do, but showed severe weakness when he had to *apply* his knowledge.

By giving children real problems to solve, we can see clear evidence of who can now do what, and where a child's weaknesses are. If we do 'closed' tasks mainly from books or worksheets, we are unlikely to see daily examples of children revealing through what they do and say that they have moved on and learnt something new – and maybe have learnt it securely enough to apply it.

Encouraging the development of mathematical thinking

One of the most noticeable things about maths lessons to be observed in many schools around the country is that it is the *teacher* who is often the one who is doing the thinking, rather than the children! A student teacher or the class teacher can be seen doing most of the talking in a group and rephrasing almost everything that children are contributing. A more effective strategy is to listen to a child's point and then either repeat what the child said in a neutral way, which hands the statement back to the child to add further comment, or ask another child also involved in the work to give his/her opinion to add to the first. Children are often given the impression that all comment must be made via the teacher and child/child interaction is not encouraged as much as it could be.

Strategies for developing mathematical thinking:

◆ Listen to children and promote talk amongst children.
◆ Keep adult intervention to a minimum.
◆ Explain through the child using concrete apparatus. If one piece of equipment fails, try something else.
◆ Let other children explain what they understand.
◆ Help the child to outline what they do know.
◆ Help the child to identify where they are 'stuck'.
◆ Develop a classroom ethos where it is acceptable to be 'stuck' and develop strategies for unsticking, e.g. outlining 'what I know' and 'what I want to know'. You could put these on the wall as 'think clouds' if you want (see page 36).

◆ Develop a classroom ethos where asking questions and not knowing the answer is acceptable. If you don't know the answer, say *'I don't know, let's find out.'*

◆ Monitor your own contributions regularly to ensure that you are using more open-ended questions than closed ones.

◆ Try not to ask the kind of question where a child knows you have one answer in your head and they have to guess it.

◆ Accept everyone's contributions and value each child. No one laughs at what others say, even if they think it is wrong. Saying *'Can you tell me why you think that?'* may well reveal logical thinking that is useful in working with the child on refining their ideas.

The curriculum that we offer children

It is probably obvious that the tasks that we plan and the ways in which we carry them out will influence the quality of our children's thinking. A headteacher told of her horror at the maths level of her Year 3 children. They had been used to using the kind of mathematical workbook where they just fill in the gaps, and had reached the age of eight unable to think for themselves or record in their own way. Maths had meant: complete the page, race onto the next book and colour in the picture. So calling it a 'mathematical' workbook wasn't quite the right word. There was almost no 'real' maths in them!

The curriculum that we offer the children will influence the conditions within our class in which we want children to achieve. It is helpful to consider the conditions that we create by asking ourselves some questions:

1   Is it **broad enough** to give lots of different experiences of the same concept? So we might do some maths from our topic work, some from a maths topic such as 3D shape, some from 'real' problem-solving situations (such as *'Our class is planning sports day this year; what shall we do?'*), some from books and some from a trip to a historical site. Creating those broad and varied experiences in which we explore maths may help children to consolidate their learning. It also sets maths in real contexts that a child can appreciate and shows maths as part of real-life skills.

2   Does our curriculum give a **variety** of **types** of maths? There needs to be relevant **practical work** (children of all ages need practical apparatus), mental maths (every day, for all children), **problem-solving** (*'Can you organise and plan the assembly/rearrange the tables in the room/plan a trip to the river?'*), **investigations** (*'What can you tell me about the number 19?'*), **use of computers** (particularly using Logo, databases and spreadsheets), **calculators** (use the calculator to find out which three consecutive odd numbers multiply together to make the number 12075), **technology** (from the simplest 'junk' model to a complex, geared model ski lift, technology is riddled with maths), **cross-curricular links** (i.e. to topics and to history, geography, art, science, technology, and the mathematical content of stories), **exposition** (teaching some facts, e.g. *'When we need to find the average number we do it like this . . .'* or pulling together some issues that have arisen in the lesson), **consolidation** (*'Who can remember how many grams there are in a kilogram?'*, *'Who can think of a different way to find the total of these two numbers?'*, *'Let's go through your tables again'*), **games** (these can often be free choice and can focus on the maths topic going on at the time or can be used to consolidate previous maths concepts), and **free choice maths** (this kind of task can be highly motivating for children and creates useful 'teacher independent' work while the teacher is working with another group). The idea is that, in the broad experiences that we will provide, there will be at least something that each child can latch onto and learn from. So if we teach fractions from a variety of types of maths, perhaps children will learn more effectively.

3   Are we offering a variety of **areas** of maths in our class? Is there a balance of number, shape, pattern, data handling, etc, and lots of ways of doing these, e.g. not all number work from a book, but also from games and from investigations?

4   Does it offer **open-ended tasks**, so that children are put in the situation where they have to think for themselves and not just fill in blanks, jump through hoops and try to remember the 'trick' of *how* to do it?

Providing opportunities for reflection

Provided that we make it clear to the children what it is that a task is for, and what we expect them to learn from it, children are able themselves to reflect on what they have done and on their own learning. They need a clear indication from us about what we are expecting, and then they need the time and space to reflect. So, for example, at the end of a maths topic on subtraction and place value, you might ask the children to reflect on some of the games and activities they have done. You might say something like *'What was the same about the "take away" game, the "three-dice hundreds, tens and units" game and the "race to a pound" money game?'*

Some children at first might be unaware of what you are asking them to comment on, but as you encourage children to make generalised statements over the months about their work, they will get better at it. A child of six commenting on subtraction might say something like *'You always count back on the number line'* or *'You always make the number smaller'*. Reflecting on place value, a child might show some indication of the importance of position (*'It matters which column you put a number in'*) or exchange (*'When you get to 10 you change it and put it in the next column'*) and grouping (*'Sometimes you exchange when you have 6 things, but mostly you exchange when you have 10 things'*).

The time to reflect and to make generalisations from learning is crucial. It helps children to identify what they have learnt, which builds up their self-esteem and helps them to feel some confidence with maths. Establishing a positive attitude in maths needs to be one of our most important goals.

The appropriate climate for learning

The classroom needs to be a secure place where children (and adults!) can be free to make mistakes and ask questions without fear of being put down. We need to create an ethos where everyone helps everyone else and where there is a deep respect for each other. What is said should be valued and every individual needs to be seen as contributing something. Where a task can be done effectively through group work, the teacher needs to plan for children to work collaboratively, taking care to structure the group to maximise learning and to give children a variety of contexts in which to learn. So a less confident child may work with a more confident one, or with another child who is shy. Other tasks may be done better with children working on their own, and quiet working conditions need to be created to enable that to take place.

It is important that children are not always grouped by ability and that the teacher should decide beforehand what she is expecting from each child. Expectations should be high for *every* child and we should recognise that children are often capable of much more than we think, if we make an effort to communicate clearly with the child and try to access their thinking.

The teacher needs to make explicit to the children some of the thinking processes and strategies that they might need for working on their maths. There could be a maths notice board where children can themselves put up some of the maths that they have been exploring. The board might include some suggestions for children to choose from, when they have some time to work on their own. The notice board could give a sense of corporate working together and, because the children feel that it belongs to them, they are encouraged to think for themselves and to explore anything that might interest them, rather than just completing the next page of the scheme. The board might have on it some 'think clouds' that clarify for the children and teacher some of the strategies that we might use as we explore maths. The teacher can make a start on these, perhaps putting up 'What to do when you are stuck – ask yourself, what do I know? What do I want to know?' Other strategies that children can readily identify are things such as 'making a task simpler', 'looking for pattern', and asking 'What if . . . ?' Children can add to these for themselves and the teacher might point out to a child what they are doing as they explore something: *'Clare, you rounded up that number, well done. That is an important strategy in maths. Could you make a think cloud and put it on the board?'*

Once children have had some experience of 'real problem-solving' (finding out about opinions throughout the age

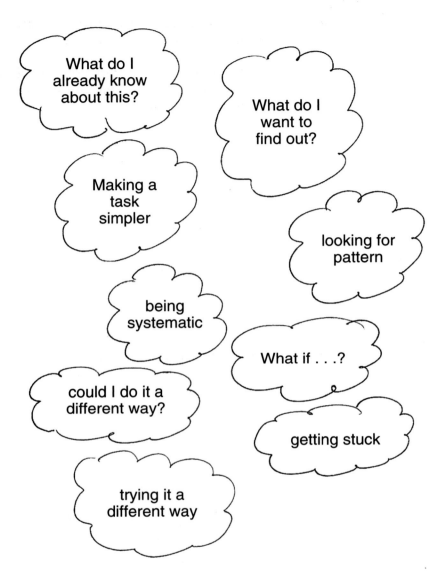

'Think clouds' of mathematical strategies and processes can focus children on to how they think mathematically.

groups in the school about smoking/drug abuse/animal experimentation/capital punishment, etc; finding the most efficient way to pack the lunch boxes tidily into the plastic crates; deciding how to reduce lost property in the school), helping them to see the kinds of processes that they go through to solve a problem can enable children to identify for themselves what they are learning and the ways in which they are improving what they do.

It can be very supportive to put up some kind of chart (see below) to clarify some of the stages we might pass through as we grapple with a problem:

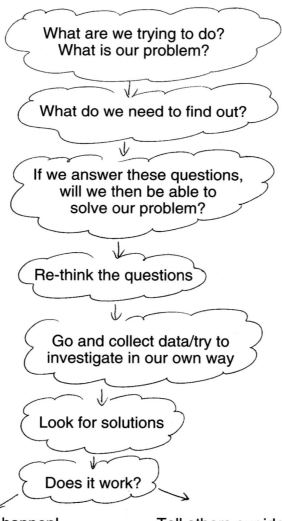

What are we trying to do?
What is our problem?

What do we need to find out?

If we answer these questions, will we then be able to solve our problem?

Re-think the questions

Go and collect data/try to investigate in our own way

Look for solutions

Does it work?

Make it happen!
(if this is a 'real' problem,
e.g. having a party)

Tell others our ideas (if this
is a mathematical
investigation)

Significant achievement in mathematics

What might this mean for maths?

It is important to have as much access as possible to children's understanding of mathematics, in order to decide whether their achievement is significant. Through the dialogue we have with children as they are working, we need to decide whether the child's understanding shows a leap, or complete understanding of a concept. Taking the five categories outlined in Chapter 1 (physical skills, social skills, attitude development, concept clicking and process skills), the following suggest some lines of development. These are very general. Chapter 3 offers a range of examples which illustrate the development in more concrete terms, and Chapter 4 provides a complete framework.

Physical skills

FROM . . .
. . . experimenting with various measuring instruments, by pushing, pulling and using them inaccurately

TO . . .
. . . being able to use them deftly and accurately (e.g. using compasses, protractors, stop watches, fine weights).

Social skills

FROM . . .
. . . talking to the teacher about their maths

TO . . .
. . . discussing and feeding back their maths with groups of other children and adults, known or unknown.

. . . being able to work alone, with short-term targets provided by the teacher

. . . working within a group and cooperatively organising the stages for themselves.

Attitude development

FROM . . .
. . . being dependent on the teacher's ideas and starting points

TO . . .
. . . being able to think of their own ideas for investigation.

. . . being dependent on the teacher's opinions about their progress

. . . being able to define their own success criteria and then provide realistic self-evaluation.

Concepts

FROM . . .

. . . recognising and understanding the symbols 0 to 9

. . . knowing that addition builds up, subtraction takes away, multiplication is repeated addition and division is repeated subtraction

. . . recognising, describing and naming the shapes and positions of things in their world

. . . being able to state a preference or opinion

TO . . .

. . . understanding the patterns in our number system and the concept of place value, both in whole numbers and numbers smaller than 1.

. . . being able to manipulate and apply the operations with any size number in any mathematical context.

. . . being able to find and calculate a variety of measures of all shapes and structures.

. . . being able to survey preferences, statistics or opinions and analyse data of the same.

Process skills

FROM . . .

. . . being given strategies and materials

. . . informing the teacher of difficulties

. . . developing their own ways of recording and representing their results

TO . . .

. . . developing their own strategies and choosing materials for any mathematical problem.

. . . identifying difficulties and modifying their strategies successfully in all aspects of mathematics.

. . . presenting their mathematics in conventional forms.

It is important that we focus not just on 'can the child do it?' (so can they subtract one number from another?), but on the attitudes that the child displays and their general ability to think for themselves. So significant achievement in maths is about the child's ability to use the mathematical thinking strategies of the think clouds (do they look for a pattern and can they work systematically?) and their ability to solve problems appropriately. It is not that facts are not important in maths, but knowing *how* to do something, such as multiplying, needs to be assessed within the much wider context of the need to know when to *use* multiplying.

Crucially, in maths, we are looking for children to be confident so that they can use what they know and work independently to get to an answer that they are happy with and that solves their problem. This is a long way from the child working to get ticks – and it is hard work to get children and parents away from being tick-oriented to focusing on developing confidence and mathematical thinking.

Creating conditions for significant achievement to occur

Pulling together some of the issues already discussed, it can be seen that there are some conditions that might influence the occurrence of significant achievement in our classrooms:

◆ praising and encouraging children;
◆ focusing on 'what did you learn today?';
◆ making clear what the purpose of the activity is;
◆ giving open-ended tasks so that the children can achieve at their own level;
◆ listening and observing;
◆ creating a classroom ethos where work is reviewed at the end of sessions, so that there is space for children to reflect on what they have done;
◆ giving children some choice in what they do.

The importance of knowing the purpose of every task

It is important in maths and in any curriculum area to know the *purpose* of every activity. What is it aiming at teaching? Of course, there might be many aims, and these can be of various types:

◆ a social aim (e.g. giving children an opportunity to work together on a cooperative task where they need to plan a division of labour to get the task done efficiently and on time);
◆ an aim to do with process skill (e.g. you might say to the children that you are giving them this task to see how well they can simplify the complex task in order to tackle it in small steps, or to see how they can think of possible ways to approach the investigation);

◆ an aim that focuses on some physical skill (e.g. *'I'm giving you this task so that you will get better at measuring things with the micrometer'*);

◆ an aim that concerns the positive attitudes that you are trying to develop (e.g. *'You all enjoyed the work with making 3-D shapes so much, I thought you might want to have more time to explore your ideas and to do some more difficult things'*);

◆ a 'concept-clicking' aim (e.g. you might say to the children that you have planned an activity about subtraction called 'what's the difference' and that it is going to help them to understand more about differences and subtractions).

One activity could have many objectives, but we need to come clean with the children and tell them what it is all about and what in particular we are looking for. Unless we do that, it is very difficult for children to engage in reflective conversation with us when we ask them how they think they got on. Children who have not being given the criteria for achievement, on being asked to evaluate themselves after a task say inconsequential things such as *'I liked the green paper'* or *'My handwriting could have been neater'*.

If we are to encourage children to become evaluators, we need to 'let them into the secret'. We need to be explicit about the reason for the child doing the task and that, later on, we will be expecting them to say how well they think they got on.

Given these conditions, children always comment on the original criteria (e.g. *'I don't need to learn my five times table because I know my tens and all I have to do is work out the tens and then halve the answer'*, or *'I think I'm good at most of the tables now, but I keep forgetting the sevens'*). This exchange between teacher and child is the vital assessment dialogue. It is through this conversation that teachers are most likely to 'spot' significant achievement.

Significant achievement and the National Curriculum

It is not necessary to track children's achievement in relation to *all* aspects of your teaching (which must be derived from the Programmes of Study, *not* the Level Descriptions). Tracking *significant* achievement, however, means that you need to have a basic idea of the big, important steps in mathematics. Chapter 4 outlines the main stages of mathematical development. However, because of the child-centred nature of significant achievement, it may be that one child takes a year to get from one stage to another. Another child, at the same time, might be progressing through a number of stages. This is where we need to redefine significance. Every small step, for the first child, shows significant achievement, and should be recorded as such. The examples of significant achievement in Chapter 3 illustrate the possible range.

The National Curriculum is designed to support the progress of a mixed-ability class. By the end of the Key Stage (the only statutory time to 'level' children against the Attainment Targets) you should expect a range of levels within the class. At Key Stage 1, the range is likely to be from W to Level 3 or even 4. At Key Stage 2 the range is likely to be from Level 2 to Level 5. As a 'best fit' approach is required, the teacher needs only consider whether, in general, a child's achievement corresponds, on the whole, more closely to one level than another. With an ongoing assessment dialogue (based on aims described in this chapter), with a scheme of work which is based on the Programmes of Study, and with the tracking of significant achievement within that framework, the assigning of levels should be relatively effortless. However, the levelling process is merely a summative snapshot of the child's attainment. It is the ongoing teacher assessment, where significant achievement is recognised and celebrated, which ensures that children will progress to the best of their ability.

References

Brissenden, T. (1988) *Talking about Mathematics*, Blackwell.
Cockroft Report (1982) *Mathematics Counts*, HMSO.
DES (1985) *Mathematics from 5 to 16*, HMSO.
PRIME *Calculators, Mathematics and Children* (The CAN Project), Simon & Schuster.
Tizard, B. and Hughes, M. (1984) *Young Children Learning*, Fontana.
Vygotski, L. S. (1971) *Thought and Language* (6th edition), MIT Press.

3 Significant Achievement in the Classroom

This chapter is the heart of the book. In it, there is a collection of work from a wide variety of classrooms showing significant achievements from children across the whole primary age range.

The work comes from different children, with differing backgrounds and different learning experiences. It illustrates some of the approaches to classroom practice outlined in Chapter 2, and it exemplifies the features of significant achievement described in Chapter 1. The examples here are not exceptional pieces of work produced in extraordinary conditions. They are ordinary pieces of classroom work, but pieces that the teacher has noticed because they are important in a particular child's development. It will be clear from these examples that something which is significant for one child may not be significant for another.

Each example starts by saying what happened – a description of what took place, or the child's work itself. It is important to remember that events which do not have children's work attached, because the significant achievement was something the child said or did, are just as significant as written work in a recording system.

Following the example itself, there are four important additional pieces of information. The first is the reason why this event was significant for this child. The second is the child's view of why it happened. The third is an indication of the type of achievement: physical, social, attitude, concept or process. Finally, the 'comment' section draws out implications for teaching, and also relates this example to other issues addressed in this book, bringing together the relationship between assessment, curriculum and significant achievement.

The examples are arranged starting with the youngest children. Examples of the different types of maths are intermingled, as are physical, social, attitudinal, conceptual and process achievements.

Richard (Reception): *Selling in the tuck shop*

The young children were finding it hard to spend their money at the playtime tuck shop because there were so many older children and they could not cope with the crush. So their teacher decided to start up an infant tuck shop. She bought large bags of crisps, biscuits, etc, at the supermarket and the children helped her to put these into small bags to sell for 3, 4 or 5 pence. She had children from five to seven in her class and she made a rota of two or three seven year olds to sell things, helped by one or two of the younger children. To her considerable surprise, some of the children in their first term were able to give change for 10p and 20p when supported by a seven year old. What she was most surprised by was Richard's ability to give change for 50p one day. (He was aged 5 and in his first term.) She observed him closely, and although the older child was beside him watching him, Richard actually did it correctly on his own.

Why was this significant?

In his number activities Richard was working with the youngest children on addition to five and matching and sorting in his maths scheme workbook. She had no idea that Richard could work with money in this way and deal effectively with numbers up to fifty. She abandoned the scheme workbook and planned a unit of work on money using coins up to 50p, and adding money up to 50p. The children coped well with it, to her considerable surprise and delight.

Why did it happen?

When the teacher asked Richard how he knew about giving change for 50p he said he had 'watched Glen and Tracy' (the older children who ran the tuck shop with him when it was their turn). The teacher said she had observed a great deal of giving change together and concluded that the younger children were learning from working with the older children. Richard's mother said that she gave him 50p pocket money each Saturday and she let him spend it on his own at the shop, so he was used to handling money.

Type: concept clicking (able to give change to 50p)

Comment

This is an example of a teacher being surprised by children's abilities and shows the need for us not to limit what our children do, but rather to expect a great deal from them and then support them in that learning.

The teacher said that she thought that a part of the reason why the children could do the number work up to 50 was that it was about real things. The use of money and the situations were real and completely understood by the children. If a bag of biscuits costs 3p and the child has 5p, they are usually well aware that they need 2p change.

Lucy (Year 1): *Learning to count on*

Lucy was doing a task in which she needed to count on, e.g. eight legs count on two more, then count on another four. Her teacher observed her count to eight, then add on the two by counting on 'nine, ten' then add on the next four, 'eleven, twelve, thirteen, fourteen' (see over).

Why was this significant?

It was the first time that Lucy's teacher had seen her count on. Previously she had always gone back to one every time.

Why did it happen?

Lucy said it was because she 'saw the crocodile' (with four legs). She was unable to say any more about it – which we might expect as, to the child, this kind of growth in her development might not be perceived as important. Her teacher observed as Lucy worked on this task that although she was supposed to be working in a group, she actually worked on her own, seeming to be motivated to do the task in her own way.

Type: concept clicking (learning to count on without going back to one)

Comment

This is a development in learning that is important in counting, and Lucy's teacher said that she would now give Lucy more experience with a number line, including work with much larger numbers.

Matthew (Year 1): *Using a calculator*

Matthew was five and in his second term at school. His teacher had thought that he could not count out accurately and did not yet have a sense of one-to-one correspondence. Consequently she was keeping Matthew (and the rest of the class) to numbers up to ten. Then a student came to the class and she and the teacher had been interested in the suggestion that giving young children calculators could improve their maths. The teacher was doubtful about this but she decided to give it a go and she set the student to work with a small group trying to make the number 2 with calculators. The student would record their work and they gave the children the examples of 1 + 1 makes 2 and 4 take away 2 makes 2.

The children set to work. (They had already had a calculator introduction session so they knew what some of the keys did.) They produced several ways of making 2 and the student asked Matthew if he had a way of making 2. He looked at her with what she described as a wicked gleam in his eye and said *'Two million and two take away two million'*.

Why was this significant?

It was an enormous surprise to both the teacher and the student. They had no idea how Matthew knew about millions (and they didn't ask him how he knew about them) but they spent an interesting whole-class discussion time exploring large numbers. They were surprised that many children could talk about thousands, etc, and many children could make a good attempt to write a large number.

Why did it happen?

Matthew was exploring numbers using a calculator and the task was not about accurate counting (a skill he had practised repeatedly with his teacher) but about something that we could assume Matthew was interested in. The open-ended nature of the task allowed Matthew to explore in his own way and demonstrate his abilities, enabling his teacher to give him more appropriate work.

Type: concept clicking (knowing the names of large numbers and a subtraction fact, but we can't know from this example how Matthew acquired that knowledge or how long he had known it for.)

Comment

This kind of example shows us how crucial it is that we don't restrict what children do in their maths. Many reception and infant classes stick to numbers up to five in the first term and to ten in the second term. But when we challenge that pattern of working and give children calculators and the chance to explore much larger numbers, we see that if we expect more from children, they often can achieve far more than we previously thought possible.

The open-ended nature of the task meant that Matthew was thinking in his own way and not just trying to find the answer that the teacher had in her head. It is an example of a young child being asked to think for himself and to begin to experience those important skills in using and applying maths that require creative thinking.

Minal (Year 1): *Fitting the jigsaw together*

14 + 18 + 18 = 50
It was a fifty piece puzzle. Minal worked carefully & got it exactly right.

Minal (age 6) was doing a task with others which their teacher had told them was a talking task: they were to find a way together to monitor the way that they put a jigsaw together. For example, they needed to work out how many times they tried to fit a piece in before they fitted it correctly. Minal worked well, organising the others, and showing a great interest in what she was doing.

Why was this significant?

This was the first time that Minal had organised a group and shown an interest in her maths.

Why did it happen?

Minal said *'Because we wanted to make good game that was fair'*.

Type: social (organising a group) and **attitude** (showed interest in her maths for the first time)

Comment

Minal's teacher said that she thought it was important to do as she had done here and make it clear to the children exactly what the criteria are, explaining these to the children at the start. So, if we want to assess something specific, then the children should know that. She also thought that *'practical and cooperative tasks need to have equal standing with formal tasks'*.

Bobbie (Year 1): *Understanding place value*

Bobbie (age 6) was playing a place-value game 'space invaders' on his calculator. To play this game you need to put a three-figure number such as 273 into the calculator, and you get rid of (or 'shoot down') one of the digits at a time. So you must enter in one single-digit number and as many zeros as you want each time to get rid of your number. So, to get rid of the 2 in 273, you must enter -200. Bobbie was trying to shoot down 2 and he realised that he could not get rid of the 2 just with entering -2. He said *'that's the hundred stage'* and saw that he needed to enter -200.

Why was this significant?

Bobbie was young to have this kind of understanding and it was the first time that his teacher had been aware of his mature understanding of place value.

Why did it happen?

Bobbie was not really sure himself how this happened. His teacher had given him a very good open-ended task. The activity focuses straight in on the major concept of the significance of the position of a digit in place value. The task involved exploring a calculator and talking about what is happening, and – as with any calculator explorations – the teacher saw the value of observing Bobbie carefully and asking him to talk about his work.

Type: **concept clicking** (the concept of the position of a digit in place value)

Comment

Although Bobbie was not able to express why he was able to do this task, it shows the crucial role of the good quality open-ended task in the mathematics classroom. Opposition to calculators is clearly there amongst the national press and education commentators, but here we see a calculator being put to the very best use (as recommended by the OFSTED reports of 1993 and 1994) and being used as a tool to explore mathematics at a level far beyond the maths of filling in boxes and doing pages of sums.

Dylan (Year 1): *Combinations of coins*

Dylan was working on different combinations of coins to make 20p. He found various ways to do this and was being systematic about it, so he was putting a ten pence then two fives, then a ten pence, one five and five one-pence coins, and so on.

Why was this significant?

It was the first time that his teacher had noticed that Dylan was working in a systematic way. She was delighted to see that Dylan organised himself in this way.

Why did it happen?

Dylan was not sure how he was able to work like this, but he was a thoughtful, fairly able and a tidy child.

Type: **process skill** (working systematically)

Comment

Observing how our children work is an important part of teaching. Because Dylan's teacher saw what he had done and was able to praise him and tell others what he had done, working systematically became an issue to talk about with the children. They would obviously need many more situations in which to attempt to work in this way, as the ability to work systematically is a crucial process in mathematical thinking.

Aklima (Year 2): *The witch's spell*

Aklima's teacher introduced the witch's spell investigation. The children needed to make some 'witch's spells' using a total of 24 legs in the cauldron. So they could have 3 spiders with 8 legs to make the 24 legs, or 4 bats (8 legs) and 4 lizards (16 legs) making 24 legs altogether, or any combination of spiders, bats and lizards.

Aklima was very motivated to do this investigation. She got very involved and started using a calculator and helping other children to understand what was going on. She quickly grasped the idea of combinations and she completed her work very quickly and with great enthusiasm, using the calculator appropriately (see over).

Why was this significant?

Aklima usually works very slowly on activities, rarely showing much enthusiasm for them, and has had considerable problems understanding the concept of combinations.

Why did it happen?

Aklima said that she had worked so well *'because I can speak more English'*.

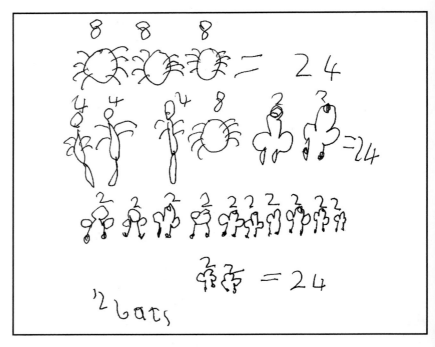

Type: concept clicking (combinations to 24), **attitude** (enthusiasm and involvement), **physical** (using the calculator effectively), **process** (working systematically), **social** (helped other children)

Comment

It is possible that, as well as Aklima's sense that she can now speak more English, she was enthusiastic about this investigation because it appealed to her imagination and maybe because her previous experiences with combinations were finally being understood. The importance of giving our children a variety of enjoyable and meaningful tasks is clear here.

Her teacher thought that she only observed this change in Aklima because on this occasion she had been sitting at Aklima's table and so was able to observe her. Her teacher decided that it was now important for her to give Aklima even more work on combinations and to combine this with some introductory work on multiplication.

Sarah (Year 2): *Doing tens and units*

Sarah (age 6) was adding tens and units when her teacher asked her why she had 'carried a ten' and Sarah explained her work, demonstrating that she understood what she was doing. Previously Sarah had demonstrated great problems in this area, clearly not understanding what she was doing.

Why was this significant?

This was new knowledge for Sarah. She understood 'carrying' for the first time.

Why did it happen?

When asked why she thought she could now understand it, Sarah said *'It's because I used the new counting rods and blocks [Dienes apparatus]. I could see what I was doing.'*

Type: concept clicking (grouping in tens, position and exchanging in place value)

Comment

Here is a teacher getting exactly the results she hoped for by introducing new maths apparatus. She sought to find some way of giving the children a varied enough set of experiences that at least something would 'click' with their mental images of what they thought they were doing in maths.

For Sarah, the new ten rods had, as far as we can tell, made some connection with what she was struggling to understand. Perhaps it was the actual physical moving of a group of ten units into the tens column, exchanging them for a ten rod that was the thing that 'clicked'. We can't know exactly what it was, as most six year olds would probably find that too complex a thing to describe. However, she knew it was the new rods and it is possible to speculate that if Sarah was asked in three or four years' time to draw what she thought was happening in some calculation such as $3456 + 6789$, or 41100 subtract 8978, she might well draw rods and blocks to represent what she understood.

This is an area in which we need more research, but what comes through clearly is the crucial need to have a wide variety of apparatus so that at least something will 'click' with each child. For Sarah's teacher there was a shared delight in the success of the new apparatus, and she realised that now Sarah needed more practical work with the new rods in order to practise her new knowledge and to extend her skills, maybe into using hundreds and considering what would happen if she did subtractions using rods and units.

Liam, Greg and Sam (Year 2): *Building a tower*

The class was split up into groups of three (Liam, Greg and Sam, all age 6) plus an older child from another class in charge of each group. The boys had the task of building a tower with large and small bricks. Previously this group had never been able to work together without fighting.

Why was this significant?

The three boys managed to complete their task with no argument. This was so different from their usual way of working that their teacher asked them why it had gone so well this time.

Why did it happen?

The boys were quite clear about why they had worked so cooperatively: *'Because we wanted to share'* (Liam), *'Because he [the older child] is my friend'* (Greg), *'Because I liked what I was doing and because of Greg's sister'* (Sam).

Type: social (working together)

Comment

The teacher had taken the time to explain to the boys that it was a 'privilege' to work with their friends and she had made it very clear at the outset that she wanted them to share and learn to work together. Making it clear what criteria we are using to assess what the children are doing is crucial. The boys were quite clear that they were meant to be sharing, so when asked why it had gone so well they focused on that, giving everyone concerned a real sense of achievement.

Working with an older child presumably played some part in the success of this group work. An older (or younger) child can have a significant influence on what children do, and maybe this is an area that we would do well to explore further in our daily work, and not only when we are concentrating on social skills.

Derek (Year 2): *Recognising odds and evens*

Derek (age 6) was working on a task on recognising odd and even numbers. This was his third session doing odds and evens and he had been unable to understand, even though he had used lots of apparatus. His teacher suggested that he draw circles around the pairs of cubes; he did that and suddenly said *'I know what an odd and even number is now because you made me draw circles around the pictures, dividing into twos and if there are none left that's an even number and I am finding out by counting in twos.'*

Why was it significant?

Despite two previous sessions when he had not seemed to understand, suddenly he could understand what he was doing.

Why did it happen?

The teacher provided Derek with a wide selection of apparatus, so that Derek was eventually able to match what he was doing with cubes etc. with the mental images he had in his mind. The drawing of the circles around the pairs seemed to consolidate for him what all the dividing into groups of two actually meant, and therefore what made an odd and even number.

Type: concept clicking (concept of odd and even) and **process** (making generalisations – working on several specific examples and then making some kind of generalised 'rule' that the child can see is true for all cases).

Comment

Derek had used a variety of apparatus and his teacher had gone on searching for a way that this task would have some meaning to Derek. By using a variety of strategies (varying the apparatus, talking to him, suggesting he draw the pictures in his mind of what he was doing) she was trying to find something that 'clicked' with Derek's mental images of what odd and even might mean. After many examples, Derek was able to make some kind of generalisation to himself, demonstrating that he had a strategy that would work for any number, however large it was.

Rachel (Year 3): *Crosses investigation*

Rachel and Tara were working together on the crosses investigation with their teacher using Cuisenaire rods. The teacher made the first and second crosses and Rachel had no problem in seeing that the second one was larger or in counting the number of little white Cuisenaire cubes needed.

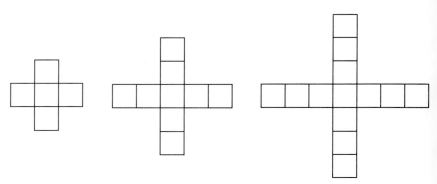

The teacher then made subsequent crosses up to the fifth cross (using the coloured rods) and Rachel was able to count up the number of little white (unit) cubes that would be needed to make each of those crosses.

Then Rachel was able to build the tenth pattern and she counted in tens to find out how many unit cubes she had needed to make it. The last aspect of the task her teacher asked her what the thirtieth cross would look like. Rachel was able to build it and, although she made an error when she calculated the number of unit cubes needed to make that pattern (she missed out one ten rod), she demonstrated that her problem-solving strategies had improved.

Why was this significant?

Rachel's strategies for problem solving had improved from the previous time her teacher had observed her. Her predictive skills, and her ability to recognise a pattern had all improved, as had her skill in breaking the problem down into simpler bits. So although Rachel had not been able to work out the numbers using multiplication as her teacher had hoped, she did show evidence of improvement in her mathematical thinking processes.

Why did it happen?

Rachel was not sure why this happened but she said she enjoyed the task.

Type: **process** (predicting the next pattern in the sequence) and **attitude** (enjoying the task)

Comment

Rachel had worked on a wide variety of types of mathematical tasks, including a range of investigations and problem-solving activities. Her teacher was using this task partly to see if Rachel would use and apply her skills of multiplications. Rachel didn't actually do that (she added up in tens, etc, rather than multiplying) but she did demonstrate an improvement in her work.

Many teachers make some kind of concluding few moments of discussion and 'review' time with the whole class. It is a time for us to say *'Rachel, you did so well on making those crosses and, Nikki, I saw how much better you were doing your written work today, and, Selina, your work with the place-value games was very good. Shall we invite your parents in to see our maths display and your investigation folders?'* It is this kind of encouragement that can make maths a subject that children enjoy, and this in turn will improve attitudes and achievement.

Jason (Year 3): *Place-value dice game*

A student teacher was playing a place-value game with a group of four 'slow learners' in maths. The children (all boys) had to throw three ten-sided dice and then place them on a hundreds, tens and units board to make the largest number possible.

Jason was struggling with the task and found it very hard to put the numbers in order. The student was making the task enjoyable and it had followed on from a previous task of making the smallest number.

The student's supervisor was observing the task and she started to write down the numbers the children were making.

763, 932, 821, etc.

Jason was still unsure about how to place his three dice and needed considerable support. When the children were picking out the largest number on the list at the end of the activity, Jason became disruptive so the supervisor asked Jason what the largest number was that he could write down. Jason said *'a million'* and wrote it down correctly. He was clearly proud of his knowledge and showed the others what he could do. The student picked up the idea and she and the children talked about what they could do if they made the hundred, tens and units board much larger and put more columns onto it.

hundreds	tens	units
7	6	3

millions	hundreds of thousands	tens of thousands	thousands	hundreds	tens	units

Why was this significant?

Although Jason was struggling to name numbers up to a thousand, he had a secure piece of knowledge about another large number. He then went on to tell the group about how many zeros other numbers had, such as ten thousand.

Why did it happen?

The supervisor was concerned that Jason was not grasping the task and he was becoming disruptive. The task was revealing what Jason *didn't* know about large numbers, but it was not clear what he *did* know. When asked how he knew how to write down the number, Jason said *'My brother showed me'* (the brother was twelve and at secondary school). He said that he did lots of maths at home.

Type: concept clicking (knowledge of large numbers) and **attitude** (joining in the discussion and stopping disruptive behaviour)

Comment

This is a good activity to teach place value and the activity went well and built on the previous work on making the smallest number. What this example demonstrates, though, is the crucial need for us to find out what children know before we set out on a unit of work with them. Children learn in any situation and they do much of that learning at home, in the park, in the playground and with other members of their family, as well as at school.

Jason knew something about large numbers, but he could not yet connect that knowledge to the activity with numbers up to a thousand. It is the teacher's job to help children to make those connections, so that isolated bits of their knowledge are gradually put together to make the jigsaw complete.

In the next activity the student did with this group, she made a long place-value board. The children made numbers with the dice and tried to name them, and Jason was good at this and enjoyed the work. He was delighted at the praise he received and was not disruptive through the whole activity – until clearing-up time!

Nicky (Year 3): *Cutting up the pizzas*

Nicky was exploring how many pieces of pizza he could make with just four line-cuts across each pizza.

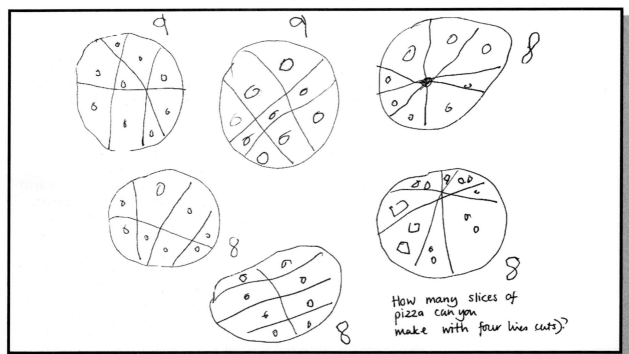

Why was this significant?

Nicky was able to stay on task and he showed enthusiasm, which was unusual for him. He usually found it hard to settle down to work and usually rushed to finish with little enthusiasm.

Why did it happen?

Nicky said that he wanted to go on and do some more. He said this was because *'I want to make more than Mandy.'*

Type: attitude (on task and working enthusiastically)

Comment

Nicky's teacher thought that part of the reason that Nicky enjoyed the activity was that the task had been set within a story context which he thought had motivated Nicky. He thought that he ought therefore to do more of that kind of contextualised task, where the maths is set in a clear story or has a reason that makes sense to the child. This links with the idea of tasks making 'human sense' to the child (Donaldson 1978).

There will always be some maths that is 'pure maths' – such as a mental maths problem adding 24 and 6, or doing a multiplication square – but usually, for primary school children, maths needs to be set within some kind of theme or story so that the children can make mental images of the task and can grasp what it is about.

In this example, the teacher could have made it quite abstract and talked about a circle being cut across with just four lines, but by making it a pizza and cutting slices, Nicky understood and worked well. The teacher concluded from this that he needed to make more maths relevant in this way and, following a whole-class discussion of what they had done, he also thought that he needed that kind of class 'review' session more frequently. This kind of review can be crucial for children's learning. They need to have help at making connections between things, and if we can build on what we have done previously we might be helping in that process. Discussion helps us to see what children already know, and makes clear what it is that they need to learn.

Jack (Year 3): *Making circle patterns*

Jack was struggling with an old-style pair of compasses to draw circles. He did not really seem to enjoy maths, but he was getting very involved in the work on circles. He was not a very coordinated child and was getting frustrated with the work as he wanted to be able to draw neat circles. His teacher told him to work on an old magazine so that the compass point had something to dig into and to move the paper around, not the compasses, as this made it easier.

Jack found that easier and he went on to produce some fascinating circle patterns and was able to describe them using good mathematical language. He made so many, both at home and at school, that he made a book of circle patterns and his teacher was so impressed by this work that she showed it to the whole school during an assembly.

Why was this significant?

It was the first time Jack's teacher had seen him persevere with a task that involved a physical skill like this. Jack's lack of coordination meant that often his work was untidy, so he tended to give up and get very frustrated and had even at times damaged other children's work that was better than his. He had severe reading difficulties but was a very bright child who joined in class discussion with great enthusiasm. For him, recording anything was difficult and the book on circle patterns seemed to be a turning point for him. He began to put in more effort and give up less easily, and his mother said that he was becoming much more settled at home and seemed to like coming to school. Through the year his reading progressed and his maths work showed his considerable abilities. His teacher was aware of how Jack's difficulties in reading often meant that he couldn't understand what he needed to do in the maths scheme.

Why did it happen?

Jack was clearly delighted with his book of circle patterns and he was proud to show it during the assembly and to put it on a colourful display of circles in the school entrance hall. Jack said he enjoyed making the patterns and he thought they were 'great'.

Type: physical (using compasses) and **attitude** (persevering and succeeding)

Comment

This is an interesting example of a child's long-term improvement in work that the teacher thought related to one significant achievement in which a child was able to experience success. It raises the important issue of the way that some children can be disadvantaged in their maths work because of difficulties not related to their mathematical abilities, in this case reading and physical coordination.

Ellie (Year 3): *Shopping and change*

Ellie (age 7) was doing a task using 1p, 20p, 50p and £1 coins and in which she had to buy about five items, add up how much they cost and report back her change from a pound. She was able to do this and reported that her list of shopping came to 60p and that she would get 40p change from a pound.

Why was this significant?

Ellie was unable to express why she was able to do this, but her teacher thought this significant for Ellie because she knew she had not taught her that there were a hundred pennies in a pound and it was the first time that she became aware of this aspect of Ellie's knowledge about money.

Why did it happen?

Ellie's teacher was giving her space to talk about her work. It is all too easy with shopping activities to let children 'just play' and to find ourselves too busy to check that they are really understanding about giving change and are able to do it correctly. (Of course, that does not mean children shouldn't play – indeed, it is essential to a child's learning that they *do* play and we need to plan that into our children's week right through the primary school.) In this situation, the teacher was monitoring what Ellie and the rest of the class were doing with great care and using a report back or 'review' session in which every child said what they had bought and the change they had.

Type: concept clicking (place value and money)

Comment

The task was open-ended and each child at review time had a chance to do it at some level. This is an example of the very best practice in whole-class teaching, where a good task can be appropriate for every child, so giving the teacher time to focus on each child and how much they are understanding. Each child would hear thirty or so other shopping lists, as every child had a chance to say what they had bought, and perhaps each child would be asked to add up the totals mentally. The children could be actively mentally calculating for almost the whole of the session.

The teacher was surprised at how Ellie knew something that had not been taught. We need to keep reminding ourselves that children are only with us for a small proportion of their lives. The fact that there are a hundred pennies in a pound might have come to Ellie during a maths game, from a question she asked at home, from a quiz programme on the television, or simply from playing with money out of mum's purse and working out for herself that if two 50p make a pound then there are 100 pennies to the pound. Ellie might not know how or when she learnt it, and it is crucial that we remember that children do not learn maths in a linear kind of way (fact A followed by fact B and then C). Children often do not learn what we set out to teach them, and they often learn *different* things from our carefully planned purposes of an activity! (No wonder teaching is so hard!)

Jonathan (Year 4): *The seven-times table*

Jonathan normally struggles with his maths and with the other areas of the curriculum, so when the teacher was challenging the class for a volunteer to say the seven-times table she was surprised to see Jonathan volunteer to do it on his own. He said it without a fault and the whole class burst out clapping. Jonathan was clearly proud of what he had done.

Why was this significant?

It was the first time that Jonathan had volunteered to say a table and he had not before known his seven-times table by heart.

Why did it happen?

Jonathan said that he had been learning his tables at home with his parents.

Type: concept clicking (learning a table, although as mentioned elsewhere, we cannot claim from this that Jonathan *understood* multiplication: what he did know were the multiplication facts of a complex and difficult table, and with time he would apply that and other tables in real-life situations and during investigative work and so learn to apply his knowledge), and **attitude** (developing confidence).

Comment

This is an interesting example of where a teacher is actively working to boost a child's confidence and self-esteem. It demonstrates too the important part parents can play in that process by giving the child one-to-one help in the security of home, where he can make all the mistakes he wants without having to face his friends.

James (Year 4): *Negative numbers*

James was doing a task about subtraction, and his teacher asked him about his results and about taking a larger number from a smaller one (see over). Much to the teacher's surprise, James started talking about negative numbers!

Why was this significant?

This was totally unexpected as they had not discussed negative numbers in class and his teacher had no idea that James knew anything about them.

Why did it happen?

James said that he had a calculator at home and he made negative numbers on that.

Type: concept clicking (knowledge of negative numbers)

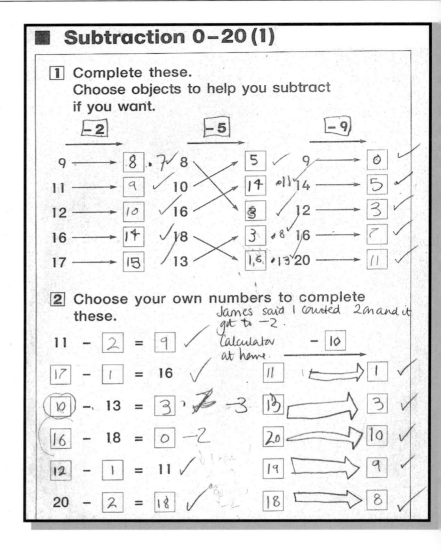

Comment

The teacher was very surprised by this and it is certainly not what we might expect a Year 4 child to start talking about. This is another example where having a calculator to explore numbers has given a child insight into maths that would traditionally be thought of as beyond their abilities.

Yuseph (Year 4): *Seeing connections*

Yuseph was recording some data about the sizes of rectangles when he seemed to be able to see connections between the numbers in the first two columns and the third one. At first he said *'Most of these are single numbers but the third ones aren't . . . because it's a bigger square.'* He began by making some connections that did not lead to much, but once he could see the link that the first and second column multiplied together gave the third column he continued to explore on his own.

Length	Breadth	number of squares
7 cm	1 cm	7 cm
5 cm	4 cm	20 cm
2 cm	5 cm	10 cm
2 cm	2 cm	4 cm
2 cm	2 cm	2 cm
3 cm	1 cm	3 cm
6 cm	2 cm	12 cm

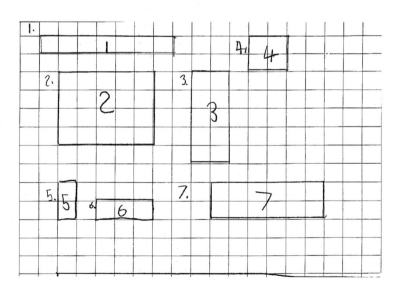

Why was this significant?

Once Yuseph was able to see some connections he went off

to get a calculator and tried some much larger numbers. He did this without the teacher asking him to.

Why did it happen?

The teacher asked Yuseph directly what he was thinking; when his teacher asked Yuseph if he could see if the pattern continued, he looked at it again and it seemed as if something just 'clicked' in him. Yuseph said *'It is just a quicker way of adding up.'*

Type: **process skill** and **concept clicking** (seeing connections between numbers, seeing a pattern, understanding that multiplication is repeated addition)

Comment

This example demonstrates the ways in which children begin to see connections for themselves. They make hypotheses about their work – not always ones that prove to be useful – and when they test these out, they are capable of independent work that they can direct. Yuseph's teacher made it possible for children to pursue their own ideas and gave them open access to the equipment, including calculators. The calculator takes the drudgery out of calculating, say, the number of little squares in a rectangle 58 by 37, enabling the child to work with many specific examples to see if their rule holds true in all cases and with large numbers.

Joe (Year 4): *Making a chart about 3-D shapes*

After a discussion about shape, Joe (age 9) was working with a group on the task of filling in a chart about the characteristics of various shapes. He took over the leadership of the group and organised them in order to get the chart filled in.

Why was this significant?

Usually Joe worked slowly, chattering as he worked, and was rarely a constructive and hard-working member of a group. It was the first time his teacher had ever observed him leading a group and keeping them on task.

Why did it happen?

Joe said he was able to work so well on this task *'because no-one else could do it'*. He had therefore taken on the role of leader.

Type: social skill and **attitude** (organising and leading a group to complete a task)

Comment

The implication for the teacher was that she saw the crucial importance of varying groups that children work in. She saw that for Joe it was going to be important to put him in a group in which he could be given more responsibility and also sometimes to put him in a group in which he might be organised by others, to observe his reactions. This kind of monitoring of a child's developments in these attitudinal and social areas might not be possible every time he works in a group, but if he is able to appreciate that sometimes he works well, he might be able to translate those good working habits into other situations, so improving his general level of achievement.

Bronwyn (Year 5): *Finding numbers that make rectangles*

Bronwyn was working with Joseph, finding which numbers can be made into rectangles and which ones can't. For example, six makes a rectangle of six by one, or three by two. She had to find out which numbers *didn't* make rectangles, as these would be the prime numbers.

Bronwyn showed considerable engagement with the task. The teacher was sitting with the group and noticed how Bronwyn was making random tries with a variety of numbers and then turning to Joseph and asking him to check what she did.

Then Bronwyn seemed to need to show that she was managing the problem on her own and said *'I need a list'*. She then worked in a systematic way and showed skills of organisation and a grasp of what she was doing. She made an accurate list, and when talking about it at the end of the task she was clear about what she had done and confident that she had found all the possible rectangles and all the prime numbers up to 25.

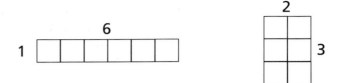

Why was this significant?

This was the first time Bronwyn's teacher had seen her use her investigative skills so systematically and in such an involved way. At first she had seemed to be a bit dependent on Joseph, but then she recognised her need to make a list and then wanted to work on her own and in her own way.

Why did it happen?

Bronwyn was clear that she needed a list, but other than that, she did not know why she was able to work so well on this task. However, the teacher said that he could see that she enjoyed the task and understood exactly what she was meant to be doing.

Type: concept clicking and **process skills** (being systematic, putting things in order, presenting results clearly, stopping and reviewing progress)

Comment

At the start of this task Bronwyn showed a need for some kind of support, and turned to Joseph for this. We often observe this kind of behaviour at the start of a task when a child is working their way into a problem, finding out if they know what to do and finding a strategy to solve their problem.

Bronwyn's teacher said that Bronwyn needed more investigative work to consolidate her skills of using and applying maths. He thought he probably needed to do this kind of work more frequently in class, in order for children to become more confident and to have plenty of experience with process skills.

Elizabeth (Year 5): *Learning times tables*

Elizabeth struggles with her maths and had been doing an activity to help her with understanding multiplication. At the end of the activity she suddenly announced *'Oh, I get it – this helps me with my tables now!'*

Why was this significant?

It was unusual for Elizabeth to express something about her maths, and for her to comment on an understanding of the purpose of the task she had been doing.

Why did it happen?

Elizabeth couldn't quite explain the reason why she had seen that it would help with tables, but said *'something just clicked'*.

Type: concept clicking (suddenly understanding something about multiplication)

Comment

We often cannot know what it is about a particular activity that 'clicks' for children. What seems likely is that some activities 'click' for children and some don't. It is therefore important that we give children a very wide range of varied practical activities and plenty of experiences with applying knowledge in contexts that make sense to them. Knowledge of tables needs to be related to contexts such as *'How many people could we get in the hall for the play?'* If the child can work out that it is possible to get 27 rows of 14 chairs, and is able to use their knowledge of multiplication to work that out, then we can say with some confidence that a child can understand multiplication. A child who can say all their tables by rote but is unable to work out a problem like the chairs in the hall cannot really be said to understand the concept of multiplication.

Jeff (Year 5): *A Logo procedure*

Jeff (age 10) was new to the school and complained that at his last school they were *'allowed to play on the computer'*. In his new class the computer was used constantly for Logo, data handling and word processing and it was timetabled through lunch times and play times so that playing 'games' was not something the children were used to. Jeff seemed not to have used Logo before and he became irritable when it was his turn to use the computer; he would not work with others who were well able to do quite complex work (as the school policy was to use Logo from the nursery onwards).

After a term he was becoming more proficient and one day he drew the space ship with Mike, using a procedure, rather than in direct mode (straight onto the screen), so he could give the computer the instruction 'space' and the rocket would be drawn.

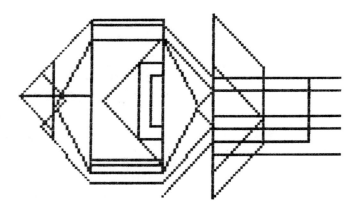

Jeff's teacher saw this as real progress and then Jeff asked if he and Mike could stay in to do something else. They worked together to make this repeating star pattern, again using a procedure. They called their drawing 'JeffMike' and they started with instructions to go forward and turn right 300 degrees, then after they had done this a few times they keyed in 'JeffMike' as a part of the procedure so that the whole procedure would be repeated and would go on drawing on the screen until it was interrupted. This kind of instruction was popular in the class and had been used to make some impressive patterns.

Why was this significant?

Jeff was clearly pleased with his work and, when asked by his teacher what he had done, he explained, revealing his understanding of Logo instructions and degrees of turn, etc, and also what a procedure could do. (Not working directly onto the screen but planning a sequence of moves that would build up into a complex picture that could be saved and used again and edited.)

Why did it happen?

Jeff said that he *'wanted to do more'* and that *'it's fun'*.

Type: process (predicting instructions needed, thinking ahead, seeing patterns), **social** (working with others) and **concept clicking** (degrees of turn, estimating distance)

Comment

Jeff's teacher said it had been an uphill struggle to get Jeff going, but that he seemed to have grasped the basics and now needed much more computer work generally – for example, he could not yet put information into a data base.

Vijay (Year 5): *Making moves*

Vijay was working on an investigation where he was trying to make the least number of moves possible. He became very involved with the task, even coping well with working with a girl!

Why was this significant?

Vijay usually hates any kind of problem solving as he assumes he will be wrong. He normally holds his head in his hands, refuses to work if the partner is a girl and shows no initiative in trying to solve a problem. He rapidly loses heart as his confidence and self-esteem are so low. Doing this task was a major breakthrough for him.

Why did it happen?

Vijay said *'I can do this in sixteen moves – I'll show you.'* He was animated and very clear about what he was doing. He drew a grid and demonstrated his work but then said *'Wait, that's wrong. Can I try it out again?'*

This was the only explanation Vijay gave, but what would seem to have happened is that for some reason this task appealed to him. Once he had achieved some success, this boosted his confidence.

Type: **social/attitude development** (becoming engrossed in a task), **concept clicking** (seeing a way to make the required moves) and **process** (drawing out a grid to clarify what he was doing and finding a systematic way of working to make the moves)

Comment

Vijay's teacher thought that the next thing she would do in maths with him would be to find a task that was almost the same and required him to think out the moves again. She thought that if Vijay could see that he had a skill which he could apply in other situations, this might boost his confidence and help him to see himself as someone who could succeed with maths.

Kevin (Year 6): *Boxes for 36 cubes*

Kevin was working on a task to make boxes that would hold exactly 36 one-centimetre cubes. He had one attempt by making a $3 \times 3 \times 3$ box, but he realised that this would not hold all the cubes. He seemed disinterested in the task. Then he watched his friend Adam make a $6 \times 6 \times 6$ box; as he watched, he could see, by mentally working out the space he needed, that Adam's box would be much too big. From this point on, Kevin became much more involved in the task and continued with his mental calculation, finally working out the size of the box he needed to make (see over).

Why was this significant?

Kevin's teacher could see that he was moving beyond the physical manipulation of cubes to mental mathematical calculation to solve his problem. The teacher noticed a 'light go on in his eyes' as one solution to the problem dawned on him, that he could work it out in his head first and calculate the exact size of the box he needed.

Why did it happen?

Kevin said that it was making his (wrong) model that helped him to 'get it'. He said that he had not understood it until he made the model.

Type: concept clicking (understanding that he could use multiplication to work out what he needed), **process skill** (using an appropriate piece of mathematical knowledge to solve a problem) and **attitude** (changed from disinterest to enthusiasm as he saw a solution).

Comment

Kevin's teacher wanted to capture this enthusiasm and to consolidate the ideas about multiplication and number patterns, so he planned to do some more investigations with number patterns.

This is another example of a good task that was challenging enough to demand considerable thinking, mental calculation, and application of knowledge.

I wanted to find out how many different boxes, We could make, that could hold exactly 36 cm² cubes.

I started of by making a 3×3 box but it Was wrong. Then I saw my friend adam making a 6×6×6 box. I thought of making one my self but then I saw that it Was wrong.

I knew it was because, I counted the base and it Was 36 Then I counted the layers and it Was six so I timed 6 by 36 like This.

$$\begin{array}{r} 36 \\ \times 6 \\ \hline 216 \\ \end{array}$$

The answer is two hundred and sixteen.
I made 5 different boxes. And all of them held 36 cm² cubes.

3×3=
2

3×6×2=36

These are two of the boxes I made.

Sam (Year 6): *Missing number sentences*

Sam had a few missing number sentences to solve, ($4 + x = 12$, $15 = x + x + x$ and $20 + x = 4 + 17$, etc) and he persevered with them and completed them accurately.

Why was this significant?

Usually Sam does not persevere but tends to give up and rarely completes a task with accuracy.

Why did it happen?

Sam said *'I'm in a good mood'* and his teacher thought it had helped him that the presentation of the first few had been good and he was able to succeed, so he got a sense of achievement. She thought this helped him to go on and work at the more complex examples.

Type: attitude (persevering with a task), possibly also **concept clicking** and **process skills** because, in this task, the attitude change seemed to lead to better work so it is possible that he was also understanding this task in greater depth and using his mathematical thinking skills.

Comment

Sam's teacher thought that he needed more of the same type of problem and then some problem solving that would put the skill in some kind of context, where he had to apply what he knew. It is not until we see a child *use* what they know in some kind of problem-solving situation that we can really be sure that the child understands a skill we have seen them practise successfully. They could just be following a formula or they might just know the 'trick'. It is only when we see a child recognise what bit of maths it is they need in a real situation that we *know* that it is 'real' knowledge and in-depth understanding and we can say with confidence that they understand it.

Clare (Year 6): *Paving stones around the pond*

Clare (age 11) rarely showed an interest in maths and persistently said *'I don't get it'* when doing any kind of investigative maths. She would sit and let the others in her group do the work. The first part of the investigation was to make the growing pattern of paving stones around the pond (see the lower part of Rupa's drawing, below).

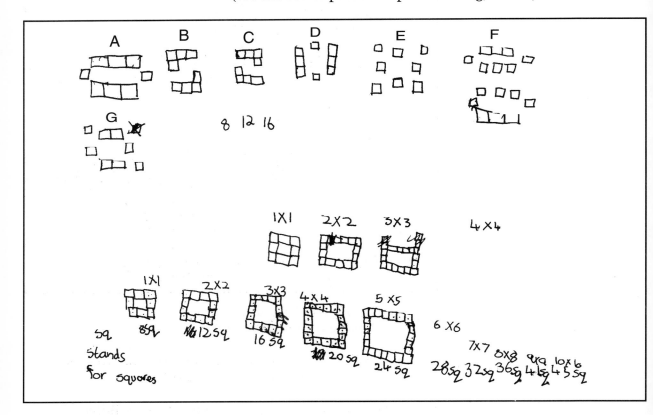

Rupa's drawing

Clare could do this and she made this recording of her work, with Rupa doing most of the work and the drawings. Then her teacher extended the investigation, asking the children to show different ways that they could 'see' the growing patterns they were making. At first Clare did her usual '*I don't get it*' then, as she and Rupa began to talk about it, Rupa made some quick sketches (see the top part of the work above).

The teacher was taking the children towards the idea that you can 'see' a pattern in more than one way, and in the whole-class discussion at the end of the session the children talked about seeing the pattern as 'two L-shapes' (see Rupa's

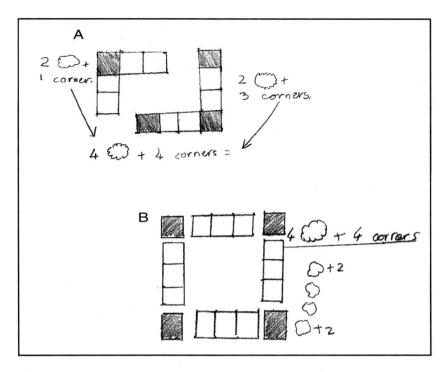

Clare's drawings

drawings B and C) and 'four sticks and four corners' (see Clare's drawing B, above) and several others.

The teacher was trying to move some of the children towards the point where they would be able to talk about some kind of generalised way of 'seeing' this pattern and she introduced the idea of a 'think cloud'. When thinking about one of the patterns, say the second pattern (the 2 × 2 in Rupa's drawing), the children said you needed four lots of the length of the side (two in this case), plus the four corners. For the third pattern (the 3 × 3 in Rupa's drawing), again you need four lots of the length of the side, plus the four corners.

So then the class went off to explore their own ways of 'seeing' in terms of the think cloud. It was then that Clare became very animated and drew two of her ways of seeing (two L-shapes and four sticks and four corners) and showed that, for each one, you needed four lots of think cloud and four corners.

Why was this significant?

Clare had never been observed showing this kind of enthusiasm for maths, nor showing that she could express what she was doing in this kind of generalised way. She took part in the whole-class discussions and seemed happy to talk about *'four lots of think cloud and four more'*. (This could be expressed as $4x + 4$ but the teacher used think clouds because it related to 'the number in your head').

Why did it happen?

When asked why she got on so well with this investigation, Clare said that her sister had shown her how she was doing her GCSE work and that she liked working with Rupa.

Type: process (seeing patterns, being able to express something in generalised terms) and **social/attitude development** (showing enthusiasm for the task)

Comment

Clare's teacher said that now Clare had 'got it' she would do a similar thing with the investigation next week and ask the children to 'see' the pattern in several ways and show that each one of those different patterns will still need the same number of 'think clouds'. She said that she would also suggest to Clare that she could tell the class about some of her sister's GCSE work. The teacher thought that this might lead to Clare feeling better about herself in maths, just as she had done this session, as Clare's low self-esteem with maths and her previous lack of positive attitude towards maths was perhaps beginning to be overcome.

Dan (Year 6): *Predicting a pattern*

Dan (age 11) found maths hard and when he was doing investigative work he seemed to hold back and not to enjoy it, so it was hard for his teacher to see what he was thinking and to talk about his work with him. His teacher wanted to give the children some experiences where their predictions of what might happen were made clear, so that they could see exactly what predicting meant. She asked the children to draw around a 2-D shape repeatedly as they rotated it along the edge of a ruler, marking the position of one of the corners of the shape each time they drew around it. They were then to join up these marked corners and look at the shape of the path that the line made. Then they were to choose another shape and try to predict the shape of the path they would make.

Dan used an equilateral triangle first, then he chose a square and said *'This will be quite smooth.'* He was quite surprised at his results and then went on to choose a hexagon, pentagon and an L-shape, each time making predictions and then talking about them with those around him.

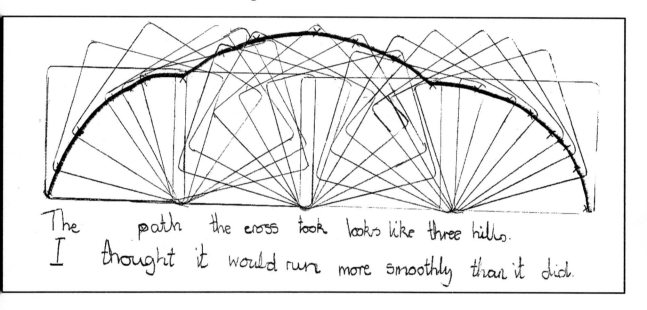

The path the cross took looks like three hills.

I thought it would run more smoothly than it did.

Why was this significant?

It was clear that Dan was well able to make predictions and understood what he was doing. During investigative work over the next few weeks, Dan was able to understand what it meant to make predictions and he seemed to be talking much more freely about his work.

Why did it happen?

When asked why he got on so well with rotating shapes he said that he enjoyed it and could 'do it'.

Type: process (making predictions) and **attitude** (enjoyment and greater willingness to talk about work)

Comment

Dan's teacher commented that perhaps she should give the children more spatial investigative work and said that when she looked back over the term she had done mostly number investigations. She thought Dan enjoyed any kind of drawing and more investigative work could help him to develop his mathematical thinking processes.

This collection of classroom events has brought out the great variety of achievements that can be significant for different children in different classes. It has also brought out the wide range of factors that have given rise to those achievements. There have been plenty of examples of sound, well-thought-out teaching, like that described in Chapter 2, clearly taking children forward. But there have also been many examples which were completely unpredictable – the influence of other children, factors from outside school, and difficulties in one area causing a lack of confidence in another, for example. In all these cases, however, it is clear that teachers have learned a great deal by talking to children about their achievements, and reflecting on what they say. The thoughtful points noted by the teachers in this chapter show the value of this approach in knowing children better and working with them to build on their achievements.

References

Donaldson, M. (1978) *Children's Minds*, Fontana.
OFSTED (1993) *The Teaching and Learning of Number in Primary Schools*, HMSO.
OFSTED (1994) *Science and Mathematics in Schools*, HMSO.

4 Development and Progression in Mathematics

Introduction

Chapter 3 gave a range of examples of significant achievement in mathematics. This chapter looks at progress in more general terms, by tracing lines of development through the different aspects of maths. Two case studies are outlined each time: one of a child at the beginning of the continuum of development, and one towards the end of the continuum. The '**From-Tos**' between the case studies draw out the different strands of development, for concepts, knowledge and skills. It is hoped that these lines of development will give some insight into what might constitute a framework for children's learning in mathematics, and thus make spotting significant achievement more manageable.

Number, Algebra and Data Handling

Lisa, *aged 5*

Lisa sings along with counting games like *'1, 2, 3, 4, 5, once I caught a fish alive'*. When asked to make some numbers on the calculator, she made and tried to write a range of big and small numbers. When asked to say what numbers they were, she simply named the numbers (e.g. *'this number is four three one and this number is nine nine nine nine nine'*) or invented her own number names (e.g. for 579835 she said *'five and seventy million hundred'*).

Observed organising a tea party in the home corner, she counted out three objects with one-to-one correspondence, counting more than three objects without one-to-one correspondence. She shared out the biscuits (six between four children) by saying *'One for you, one for you'*, etc, and then said she would save the other two for later. In cooking, she said that the left-over jam tarts could be cut in half. She was able to cut them in halves, showing that she understood what a half was.

There is a class collection of buttons, which Lisa can sort in various ways (e.g. by number of holes, shiny and not shiny). This arises from the teacher asking her to choose one she likes, then sorting other buttons which are like this from those which are not.

She can make simple repeating patterns with Unifix or beads and likes body pattern games (e.g. stand up, sit down, stand up, sit down, etc).

FROM . . .

. . . recognising and understanding the symbols 0 to 9
being able to read the numbers aloud, say them in the right order when counting objects, know that each number is one bigger than the last.

. . . seeing simple repeating patterns in colour, shape and number
e.g. red, yellow, red, yellow bead or Unifix pattern, 123, 123, 123 and square, triangle, circle, square, triangle, circle.

. . . knowing that addition builds up, subtraction takes away, multiplication is repeated addition and division is repeated subtraction
using the addition button on the calculator to add more to a number or getting more cubes to make the total number of cubes bigger; using the subtraction key to make a number get smaller or taking cubes away; knowing that 6×3 is $3 + 3 + 3 + 3 + 3 + 3$ and that to find out, therefore, how many tiles would fit on the wall, they would need to be counted in rows and columns; knowing that $70 \div 10$ is $70 - 10 - 10 - 10 - 10 - 10 - 10 - 10$ and that to share 24 biscuits between 4 people, you find how many sets of 4 can be taken from 24.

. . . being able to state a preference or opinion
e.g. *'I like coke better than orange'* or *'They like it because all their friends like it'*.

. . . being able to say whether real-life events are possible or impossible
know that it is *possible* that the Queen would come to the school, *impossible* to get younger and *certain* that you need food to live.

TO . . .

. . . understanding the patterns in our number system and the concept of place value, both in whole numbers and numbers smaller than 1

know the patterns when jumping in 10s, 100s and 1000s from any number, forwards or backwards, know that the numbers move around the decimal place according to their size and know relationship between whole-number positions and numbers after the decimal place (e.g. 100s, 10s, 1s etc).

. . . understanding and creating formulae for calculating various situations

finding the area of various rectangles, then creating a formula such as $l \times w$, looking at a growing pattern and working out the formula for any number in the sequence.

. . . being able to manipulate and apply the operations with any size number in any mathematical context, with or without a calculator

use any of the four operations in **real-life problems**, e.g. *How much fencing do we need for the new playground?*, *How much will the coach trip cost?*, *How can we find out how much water will fill the pond?*, and **pure maths problems**, e.g. *Start with any number; if it is even double it, if it is odd subtract 1 – continue with each new number and see how long it takes to reach 0. How many combinations are there for colouring in the flag in four colours? Create your own magic square.*

. . . being able to survey preferences, statistics or opinion and record and analyse data of the same

designing a collection sheet then carrying out a survey about (e.g.) children's opinions about pocket money, then collating the data and recording it graphically, and finally analysing the results so that there is a conclusion.

. . . having a secure understanding of probability

be able to decide whether the probability of an event can be calculated (e.g. the chance of getting a 6 on a die) or whether it must be based on previous experience (e.g. the outcome of a football game, which would depend on the team's previous record, etc).

Ben, *aged 11*

Ben was asked to make the number ten in as many ways as possible, using addition, subtraction, multiplication and division and using big numbers and decimal numbers where appropriate. The following are extracts from his number sentences:

$4 + 6$	$1000 - 990$	2×5
$3 + 7$	$1010 - 1000$	3×3.3333333
$9 + 1$	$1020 - 1010$	4×2.5
	$1030 - 1020$	5×2
		6×1.6666666

He has done lots of number-line jumping exercises, jumping in tens and hundreds from any number backwards and forwards, using the 0 to 1000 number line which is mounted along the corridor. As a result of these, he can say the numbers without the number line, both orally and in his head (e.g. *'Start from 7, jump in hundreds and say the numbers aloud'* – *'7, 107, 207, 307, 407, 507 . . .'*; *'Now try in thousands'* – *'7, 1007, 2007, 3007, 4007 . . .'*

He was recently involved in a group problem-solving exercise in which they were trying to design the playground before the playground painters came. Ben conducted surveys of opinion across the age groups and showed graphs of his findings. Together the group drew several scaled designs of the different courts and playground games, then asked children in the school to sign against their preferences. These were tallied and more graphs produced. Ben was able to say which designs were most popular for the different age groups.

Ben's work in measures has led him to create formulae. For instance, in working out which of a number of boxes held the most cubes, he worked out the formula for calculating volume. In a pure maths investigation he worked out the formula for the growing pattern.

Shape, Space and Measures

Nadia, *aged 5*

Nadia can match 3-D shapes when 'posting' them into a shape box. She knows what a square and a triangle look like, and can name them, but sometimes calls a rectangle or even a cuboid a square as well. When she plays the 'Feely Bag' game (describing a shape to someone else for them to guess) she uses words like *'flat'*, *'straight'*, *'corner'*, *'pointy'* and *'round'* and some real-life comparisons, like *'box'* and *'ball'*.

When Nadia plays with the class doll's house and on the construction apparatus, she uses positional words mostly appropriately (e.g. *'inside'*, *'next to'*, *'behind'*).

Nadia plays with the measuring instruments on the maths table and can approximate measuring with them (e.g. uses the tape measure to 'measure' something, but invents the number). She can make simple comparisons when asked to order objects by saying that one thing is bigger, longer or heavier, but gets muddled with 'wide' and 'narrow'. When asked to put the ribbons in order of length, she placed them in a line, and mostly in order, but did not line them up at their lower edges:

In a class discussion about how far it was from the classroom to assembly, Nadia said it was probably *'ninety hundred steps'*.

FROM . . .

. . . experimenting with various measuring instruments, by pushing, pulling and using them inaccurately
using ruler lengths to measure distance, using a tape measure to measure someone's arm, but not being able to read off the correct number, pressing down on the kitchen scales and noticing that the pointer moves over the heavier the object is.

. . . being able to make basic comparisons of size and quantity
saying that one thing is smaller, bigger, lighter, heavier, longer, taller, etc, than another.

. . . recognising, describing and naming the shapes and positions of things in their world in their own language
using words like *'box'*, *'diamond'*, *'pointy'*, *'rounded'*, *'side'* when playing.

TO . . .

. . . being able to use them deftly and accurately (e.g. using compasses, protractors, stop watches, fine weights)
use appropriate measuring instruments accurately and in the appropriate situation, e.g. using a protractor to plot a treasure map or a stop watch to time pulse-rate after exercise.

. . . being able to find and calculate a variety of measures of all shapes and structures
being able to measure accurately using standard units, both imperial and metric, and use understanding of the different measures when solving problems such as *How much orange do we need for the class picnic?* or *Find out how much wood is needed for the shelf.*

. . . using conventional shape names and shape language for most 2-D and 3-D shapes and being able to construct them in both dimensions
knowing regular and irregular shapes, such as hexagons, pentagons, octagons and cube, cuboid, tetrahedron, etc, shape language such as *'face'*, *'vertices'*, *'perpendicular'*, *'parallel'*, etc, and be able to create a triangular prism from straws and plasticine.

Naseem, *aged 11*

Naseem can name all 2-D and 3-D shapes. In playing 'Make the same shape' (two children sit on either side of a screen with a pile of identical shapes – one makes a construction of the shapes then describes it carefully to the other, who has to try to construct the identical shape), Naseem used appropriate words, such as *'edge'*, *'face'*, *'vertices'* as well as *'left'*, *'right'* and approximate angles.

He can construct simple shapes with given angles using a ruler and a protractor and compasses.

When the class was involved in designing the roof garden for the school, Naseem used his knowledge of most aspects of measures in problem-solving, demonstrating his understanding of the concepts. For instance, he worked out how much soil would be needed to fill the large planters, how much turf would be needed for the grass area and how much fencing would be needed. He also looked in the local garden centre catalogues in the classroom and calculated which was the best value overall.

He can use imperial and metric measures and measures accurately, according to the measuring instrument he is using.

5 Some Common Questions Answered

This chapter deals with the common questions that have emerged from teachers beginning to track significant achievement.

▶ **Does this fulfil the statutory requirements for assessment and for OFSTED?**

Yes. The statutory requirements are that assessment and record-keeping must be done in relation to the core attainment targets, but the amount of assessment and recording and the form of records is entirely up to teachers, taking account of good practice and manageability The SCAA/DFEE Assessment Arrangements state that collections of evidence are not required, nor tick lists for each child against the criteria of the National Curriculum. You may receive guidelines from LEA advisors or inspectors asking you for some of these things, but the actual statutory requirements are as outlined here.

The significant achievement system fulfils the statutory requirements, with the tracking matrix ensuring tracking against the attainment targets of the National Curriculum.

▶ **How do you record coverage and achievement across the whole of the maths curriculum?**

The Assessment Arrangements for Key Stages 1 and 2 point out the requirements, which are reflected in what follows. Your detailed planning gives you a good picture of the range of experiences that have been provided for the children in your class. If work has been appropriately differentiated, you will also have an idea of the child's capabilities. The child's ongoing classroom work and your marking comments will be another valuable indicator of particular strengths and weaknesses across the maths curriculum.

Each child's Record of Achievement (if you choose to keep them, as they are not statutory), containing examples of significant achievement, will show the kind of progress a child has been making, the quality of the work, the child's views on his or her significant progress, particular conditions that support learning and ways forward. These sources of information will provide you with more than enough material to help you plan future learning experiences or report on progress. See the SCAA/DFEE Assessment Arrangements booklets for the statutory requirements for assessment, in which they point out a number of times that you are *not* required to keep detailed checklists or collections of evidence, but rather some form of assessment and record-keeping which tracks progress against the aspects of the Programmes of Study only (e.g. reading, writing, speaking and listening, handwriting, spelling, number, using and applying, shape, space and measures, etc).

▶ How many times do you have to see significant achievement to write it down?

You need to define the significance. For instance, it might be significant for a child to hold her pen properly for a short period of time and should be recorded as such, even though she may go back to holding it wrongly afterwards; it is at least a first step. The next significant achievement for that child would probably be when you notice that she is now holding the pen properly all the time. Recording significant achievement has a formative purpose – it aims to support the teacher in planning the next step for the child. This is quite different from the summative tracking of attainment in relation to the old Statements of Attainment. Then you were being asked to consider children's abilities against set criteria, which took no account of an individual child's progress towards certain goals.

▶ **I have some bright children who always get everything right in their maths. Does this mean they never have significant achievement?**

This is a common comment by teachers when they first start tracking significant achievement. Brighter children should be showing as much significant achievement as less able children. However, it does mean that the teacher has to make sure that she is providing challenging learning experiences in mathematics to enable significant achievement to occur (see Clare's (page 79) think clouds for a good example of this in Chapter 3). Simply ploughing through pages of skill practice in maths is something which many children can master and appear to have no more to achieve, but we can only really believe that children understand particular maths concepts if they can *use* them in problem-solving. There are also all the social skills and processes involved in, say, organising group problem-solving or investigations. Teachers trialling significant achievement found that they often needed to revise their plans and go back to the maths Programmes of Study to ensure that brighter children were being stretched.

▶ **I don't find it easy to spot examples of concept clicking.**

Many teachers find it difficult to know what the conceptual development for mathematics consists of. The Programmes of Study do give the main concepts, but, as mentioned before, it is only when a concept such as multiplication is applied in open-ended problems that you can be sure that a child really has grasped it (e.g. uses multiplication to find out how many seats will fit in the hall). The development of concepts takes time and very rarely happens as the result of one experience. In the early stages of developing concepts children might just be making connections between one aspect of maths and another, and only gradually will they be able to generalise over a range of situations. Some of the strategies outlined in Chapter 2 for finding out children's ideas are useful for being clearer about children's understanding.

▶ I find it difficult to know who's done what when they do problem-solving and to keep track of a child's steps

Try creating short-term targets as a way of structuring problem-solving, and present them as a poster in the classroom. For example:

Stages of problem-solving:

1. *What do you think the answer will be?*
2. *What materials will you need to solve the problem?*
3. *How will you work it out?*
4. *Have a go, keeping a record of your results.*
5. *Change your method or your materials if it goes wrong or you change your mind and think of a better way.*
6. *Keep going until you are satisfied with your results. Compare your answer with your prediction.*

These stages can be used as intervention points. For example, first ask children to spend about two minutes predicting what the answer will be, and to write this down or come to tell you. Then ask them to spend about five or ten minutes looking at the maths resource area and deciding what things they might need, and so on. This keeps the children very well focused and gives you an opportunity to interact and notice when significant achievement occurs. It also gives support to children's recording of open-ended problems.

▶ How can I support and assess bilingual pupils?

Many of the suggestions in Chapter 2 for creating a positive climate for learning mathematics provide a vital starting point in supporting bilingual pupils. First and foremost it is important that bilingual pupils feel that their language and culture are valued in school and that they have work that is appropriately challenging. In planning and organising activities, it is helpful to consider the following:

◆ Is there scope for bilingual pupils to use their first language?

◆ In what ways does the activity build on existing knowledge and understanding?

◆ How can the activity be introduced so that it is accessible to all? – consider the use of diagrams, demonstration, models, practical resources, gestures, pictures, tapes, display.

◆ Which key words would it be useful to translate and reinforce through display, diagrams or games? Make sure you identify, use and reinforce the same words each time, so that children can follow the strands in your talking.

◆ How will bilingual pupils contribute and record? Can they do this in their first language? Would tables or diagrams be useful?

◆ Is the grouping supportive – allowing use of first language, including a supportive friend or a competent user of English?

◆ How can the activity extend the child's linguistic ability?

▶ **What do you do about a child who is not showing any significant achievement?**

This shows that you have a good monitoring system (Chapter 1 talks about a summative tracking matrix). First of all, perhaps it is just that you have not noticed what the child is doing (teachers said that, to begin with, they only noticed very obvious significant achievement, then the brighter and the less able children, and that 'middle ability' children are always the most difficult to track). It could also be that you are looking for something too spectacular. Significant achievement is anything which you think would be important to write down about a child.

Teachers pick up children's responses in a variety of ways, through questioning, class discussion, children's recording or observations of how children work. However, some (often quiet) children seem invisible. It is worth planning to watch the child more closely. Track the child through the day or a week. What does the child do? Is the child involved in discussion or activities? Who does the child work with? Where does the child position him/herself? Who does he or she talk to? Is the child, in fact, making very small steps forward? Talk with the child during activities; does the child understand the purpose of the tasks that have been set? Ask the child about his/her likes/dislikes or where he/she feels confident/unconfident. This may give you some clues about what is going on. Involve other colleagues and any support staff who work with the child. Talk with parents, if appropriate.

Sometimes this investigation will produce some kind of answer – for example, a need for support or extra challenge in a particular area, the need to rearrange class groupings or tackle problems in the playground. It might suggest areas of special interest or confidence that you can build on. One teacher found that, after half a term, there were four children for whom she had found no significant achievement. Her strategy was to take each of the children aside and look through their work with them. She found, by doing this, that they had indeed made progress. The teacher then wrote some retrospective event sheets and comments on the children's work, which gave them a tremendous boost of morale. For the teacher, it was a learning experience to see that for those children the progress had been missed but was in fact in evidence.

All children should be demonstrating significant achievement, regardless of their abilities. It is simply a matter of redefining significance for that child. Very tiny steps for one child are just as significant as big, more obvious steps for another.

▶ How do you get time to talk to the children?

It is important that the idea of significant achievement is *not* seen as something *separate* or *added on* to normal classroom practice. Discussion about learning intentions and significant achievement needs to be built into the usual times we talk to children – when we introduce tasks, talk with children about their work, handle feedback sessions, manage class sharing time, mark work, etc. Then the question becomes: How do you get time to talk to children in general? Teachers spend most of their time talking to individual children in the classroom, whether they are sitting in a group or answering questions or being brought finished work. These are the natural times for an assessment dialogue to take place; it is a matter of simply changing the emphasis of the things you say, including questions about the child's views on progress in terms of the shared learning intentions (see Chapter 1) as well as the usual management or supportive general statements.

▶ **Do you need to moderate significant achievement, so that we all mean the same thing by it?**

The purpose of moderation processes is to establish common definitions of each level of the attainment targets within the context of children's work, to ensure greater confidence in teachers' own assessments at the end of the Key Stages.

Moderation is only appropriate where there is a set of criteria, as in the National Curriculum level descriptions, which will be used to create levels for each child at the end of each Key Stage.

In tracking significant achievement, however, although your basic framework, for most children, will be the National Curriculum Programmes of Study, there can be no benchmarks defining stages of significant achievement. There is no need to embark on moderation of significant achievement because each teacher is in the best possible position to decide what constitutes significance for each child. One child's range of significant achievements may only take them a small step along the development set out in the programmes of study, whereas another child might have an equal number of significant achievements, but end up much further along the way. Very often your criteria for significant achievement will not be found in the programmes of study anyway, but are significant because they help the child along the continuum of learning in all its aspects.

It is, however, very useful to get together as a staff and share examples of significant achievement so that you can build up a clearer picture of what achievement might look like for a particular child or in a particular subject area. (See Chapter 6.)

▶ What do you show parents?

The child's record of significant achievement provides an invaluable focus for discussion at parents' evenings. It gives a picture of the whole child, shows developments that have taken place across the curriculum, and indicates the next steps that need to be taken. It can be very useful in helping parents to appreciate what constitutes progress in each subject. Schools also need to continue to produce end of year reports which summarise progress over the previous year.

Some schools place a marker (e.g. red felt pen mark) in the top right corner of any page of a child's workbook which has a significant achievement comment on it. This gives easy and instant access to significant work in children's books, both for parents and teachers.

▶ How would you carry out agreement trialling with the National Curriculum level descriptions?

The level descriptions are intended to be used by applying 'best fit'. The idea is that you consider the whole range of a child's achievements and decide which level for each attainment target best fits a child's achievements. This should not be an exact fit, but rather the one which best corresponds to what a child can do overall.

In order to develop a common interpretation of the levels, one strategy is for each teacher to bring one child's work for the agreed attainment target to the agreement trialling meeting, with a page of prepared notes summarising the kinds of things the child can do which are ephemeral (not written down by the child but corresponding to the criteria in the level descriptions). In pairs or fours, teachers take one child's work at a time and decide what level is most appropriate and why it cannot be the next level. Groups move around the room looking at the work until all groups have seen all children's work (about four children's work for a one-hour meeting). At the end, the groups compare their judgements, opening the debate to decide the majority opinion. Any problems which occur about decisions or interpretations of the level descriptions can be taken up with local education authority advisers or SCAA subject officers.

There are, of course, other approaches to agreement trialling.

▶ What would a School Portfolio look like?

The purpose of the school portfolio is to provide evidence of the school's agreed interpretations of the levels. The idea is that the work agreed at agreement trialling meetings is simply placed in a folder of some kind. This can then be shown to moderators, parents, governors, new teachers or any other interested parties.

If you decide to moderate using whole collections of work from one child, the portfolio could consist of plastic punched wallets, one for each level of the core attainment targets, so that lots of work from one child can be shown for each level. This work would obviously have to be put into the folder at the end of the year when the child is no longer using it, so a reference sheet could be placed in the wallet until then.

The portfolio could also consist of a large file, with work simply stored in the file between dividers for each attainment target and for each level.

There should be, for each collection for each level, a brief note about the level decided and why it did not fit the next level up. It should also include the date of the meeting.

▶ What about the end of Key Stage and the allocation of levels?

At the end of the Key Stage your planning records, the child's work, your marking, the record of achievement and your informal observations of their progress will give you ample evidence on which to base your judgements of a child's level. These sentiments are echoed in the SCAA Assessment Arrangements booklets.

6 Getting Started

The previous chapters have discussed ways of promoting and identifying significant achievement in mathematics and have examined examples from the classroom. The question then is: How do you get started? How can you begin to track significant achievement in your class or school? How do you create the conditions for significant achievement to occur? This chapter offers some suggestions based on the experiences of teachers who have been involved on courses on significant achievement.

Getting started: some general principles

In planning the introduction of any change or new development, such as tracking significant achievement, the following general principles are useful.

Build on what you are doing already

Many elements in the approach to tracking significant achievement discussed in this book are not new. The approach draws on many developments in primary practice over the last few years, for example:

◆ a more consistent approach to planning;
◆ the increased recognition of the need to clarify learning intentions;
◆ the involvement of the *child* in assessment, for example through the *Primary Language Record* (CLPE 1988) or the use of self-assessment sheets in mathematics;
◆ development of pupil profiles and Records of Achievement;
◆ the discussion of dimensions of learning, as for example in *Patterns of Learning* (CLPE 1990).

As a result, there may be many aspects of your current practice that you value and can build on. It is therefore important to begin by reviewing what you do already as a school or class, and considering how it could be extended or modified.

Start small

Trying to introduce a complete change in practice overnight is a daunting prospect and rarely effective. Starting small gives teachers the chance to experiment with different approaches and techniques, share problems and evolve an overall system that fits their own school policies and situation. You could begin with a small pilot project on significant achievement: tracking significant achievement in your class for a few weeks, concentrating on one area of the curriculum or involving a small group of interested teachers. Some teachers have introduced the idea of significant achievement to their schools by working with interested colleagues and then gradually involving the whole staff.

Begin with areas of strength and extend outwards

In taking on any new idea, building on areas of strength gives you the best chance of success. Many teachers when starting to consider significant achievement have begun by concentrating on language development, as this is the area in which they feel most confident and have the clearest view of children's progress. They have then extended the same approach to other areas of the curriculum.

Make time for regular review

As new practices are introduced and implemented, ideas often change and develop. Further suggestions emerge or unanticipated problems occur. People can become discouraged by difficulties or lose focus once the initial enthusiasm wears off. Planning opportunities to review what has happened and share experiences can enable teachers and children to refine their approach, regenerate commitment and have a sense of their own progress with this new venture.

Getting started: examples of practice

Over the last year teachers have shared with us the differing ways in which they have introduced the idea of significant achievement in their classes and schools and begun to develop their practice in mathematics. The following suggestions are based on their ideas and experiences.

Getting started with your class

In the early stages, teachers reported that they had tried to promote and identify significant achievement in their classes by:

Focusing more explicitly on learning intentions

◆ clarifying learning intentions at the planning stage;
◆ sharing learning intentions with the children in a variety of ways – through talk, writing, display and questioning;
◆ planning time to review learning with the class and individuals.

Introducing the idea of significant achievement to the class

◆ talking with the class about significant achievement;
◆ sharing examples of children's work over the last year, since they came to school or from the infants/nursery – discussing how the examples differ, e.g. more accurate recording, use of measurement, increase in number or quality of explanations or questions;
◆ making decorated sheets and folders to record and store examples of significant achievement;
◆ setting up a display or noticeboard about significant achievement, linking this to learning intentions;
◆ establishing a sharing time for children to talk about things they are proud of.

Tracking significant achievement

◆ monitoring significant achievement for a month, examining the pattern for individuals and areas of the curriculum (using the grids from Chapter 1);

◆ identifying individuals or areas of the curriculum that need further attention.

Taking time to discuss children's work

◆ making notes of significant achievement on children's work *at the time*;
◆ referring back explicitly to learning intentions;
◆ indicating not just *whether* the work was good or not, but *why* and *in what ways*;
◆ drawing attention to positive examples of work both during and after sessions.

Involving children in decision-making

◆ sharing ideas for planning at the start of a project or activity;
◆ discussing improvements in classroom resources and their organisation;
◆ explaining the need to talk with groups or individuals about their work;
◆ talking about how children can help and support each other.

Considering the whole child in context

◆ focusing on the development of skills as well as knowledge and understanding;
◆ recognising the importance of attitudes and approach to learning;
◆ examining classroom groupings more critically;
◆ considering the involvement of parents.

Reviewing progress

◆ encouraging children to identify their own significant achievements;
◆ getting feedback from children about the effects of focusing on significant achievement – many noted a considerable increase in confidence and self-esteem;
◆ noting individuals *not* making significant achievement;
◆ sharing successes and progress with the class.

Getting started with the school

Teachers used a number of different strategies for introducing the idea of significant achievement in their schools. They:

◆ introduced the idea of significant achievement using the framework described in Chapter 1;
◆ shared examples of significant achievement from their own classrooms or the course;
◆ asked teachers to bring their own examples of significant achievement to a staff meeting, sharing ideas and difficulties and identifying common patterns;
◆ reviewed current practice in planning, assessment and record-keeping;
◆ discussed ways of building a focus on significant achievement into aspects of current practice, e.g. planning cycle and proformas, current observation and sampling procedures or systems of record-keeping;
◆ trialled the approach for half a term, identifying groups/areas of the curriculum where significant achievement is often not observed;
◆ planned INSET to focus on areas of concern, for example mathematical or scientific investigations, extending able pupils, and assessing bilingual learners;
◆ exchanged examples of progress regularly, both formally and informally;
◆ discussed what should be passed on to the next teacher, each teacher bringing a child's Record of Achievement to a meeting and swapping records with a colleague, deciding what would be useful.

Developing maths in the classroom

In trying to promote significant achievement in mathematics, teachers indicated that they were:

Doing more investigative work and problem-solving

◆ starting with contexts which are meaningful and purposeful or are interesting mathematically;
◆ doing a problem with the whole class together, with groups taking different aspects or children working at their own level;

◆ finding good resource books for ideas (e.g. BEAM materials);
◆ getting cross-curricular problems from topics;
◆ trying not to tell children how to do the problem, but asking questions which help them to try out their own ideas.

Ensuring that the working ethos is supportive

◆ having lots of sharing sessions, where children report back on what they have done and how they did it;
◆ making sure that *all* methods are valued, by not saying which person's method is 'best' or quickest;
◆ explaining to children that they need to try things out and that things might go wrong which will lead to them changing their method.

Organising mathematical resources to enhance the learning

◆ setting out basic maths equipment (e.g. number lines, counting equipment, calculators, measuring devices) in boxes on an accessible surface, and encouraging children to 'look at what resources you might need';
◆ having different types of paper available, especially for data handling, so that children can choose what they think will be appropriate. The resources then become part of the problem-solving process;
◆ having a 'puzzle of the week';
◆ displaying children's maths work, with captions inviting children to find other ways of solving the problem or to think of related problems they could solve themselves.

Looking more carefully at the resources in the school

◆ making sure that the activities are not just getting children to plough through skills they have already mastered, but are asking them to apply those skills;
◆ checking activities for readability and simple instructions;
◆ checking games for simple rules rather than rules which mean the game is so complicated another adult will be needed;
◆ checking scheme books to make sure that they encourage

a range of methods for calculation, and not just standard algorithms;

◆ throwing out maths activities which slow down children's mathematical development.

Involving parents

◆ displaying a planning poster with learning intentions clearly indicated;

◆ organising a parents' evening to explain about the school's approach to mathematics, or, if these are not well attended, making sure this is communicated on open days/evenings;

◆ publishing a booklet for parents about the importance of investigative work and the place of standard algorithms;

◆ setting up a classroom display of significant achievement in mathematics;

◆ sharing examples of significant achievement with parents, both informally and formally.

Only you and your immediate colleagues can decide how best to apply the principles involved in tracking significant achievement in your own class or school. It is important that you let these principles guide the style and formats you adopt for recording purposes, rather than making the recording system the first point of reference. And although the approach to assessment outlined in this book more than satisfies statutory and inspection demands, some educationists and others will always ask for paper-and-pencil statistics, in order to satisfy their own agendas. We must make sure that they do not lead us to focus on meaningless marks on paper, when our duty is to help to further children's **learning** *to the best of our ability.*

Some useful resources

Recording children's achievements

Primary Language Record: Handbook for teachers, published by Centre for Language in Primary Education (CLPE), Webber Row, London SE1 8QW.   This wonderful handbook gives a helpful outline of record keeping and is appropriate right across the curriculum.

Open-ended mathematical activities:

BEAM (BE A Mathematician) publish very good materials for teachers that are written and trialled by teachers. For a catalogue write to Sheila Ebbutt, BEAM orders, Barnsbury Complex, Offord Road, London N1 1QH tel. 0171 457 5535 fax 0171 457 5906.

Manchester Mathematics Resources Group publish small booklets of starting points for maths for children from 5 to 16.   Many booklets are under £2 and they are excellent value as they supplement any scheme of work. Write to Gillian Hatch, Manchester Metropolitan University, Faculty of Community Studies, Law and Education, 799 Wilmslow Road, Manchester, M20 8RR.

New Cambridge Mathematics is a maths scheme that uses many open-ended activities and integrates calculators and computers. Other Cambridge materials include Anita Straker's *Talking Points* and her mental maths books. For details of all Cambridge materials write to Cambridge University Press, The Edinburgh Building, Shaftesbury Rd., Cambridge, CB2 2RU or ring the marketing department on 01223 325013

Other helpful books

Mathematics with Reason, Sue Atkinson, published by Hodder and Stoughton.

The ***Managing Primary Mathematics*** series (editor: Shirley Clarke), published by Hodder and Stoughton:
Developing a Scheme of Work for Primary Mathematics, Sue Atkinson
Discovering Mathematics with 4 to 7 Year olds, Anna Lewis
Teaching Measures: Activities, Organisation and Management, Janine Blinko and Ann Slater.
Enriching Primary Mathematics with IT, Janet Ainley.